Lucky Bastard

Lucky Bastard

My Life, My Dad, and the Things
I'm Not Allowed to Say on TV

JOE BUCK

with Michael Rosenberg

DUTTON

DUTTON

An imprint of Penguin Random House LLC
375 Hudson Street
New York, New York 10014

LIBRARY OF CONGRESS CATALOGING-IN-PUBLICATION DATA
Names: Buck, Joe. | Rosenberg, Michael.
Title: Lucky bastard : the story I can't tell on TV / Joe Buck, with Michael Rosenberg.
Description: New York : DUTTON 1852, [2016] |
Identifiers: LCCN 2016011271 (print) | LCCN 2016040924 (ebook) | ISBN
9781101984567 (hardcover) | ISBN 9781101984581 (trade paperback) | ISBN
9781101984574 (eBook)
Subjects: LCSH: Buck, Joe. | Sportscasters—United States—Biography.
Classification: LCC GV742.42.B855 A3 2016 (print) | LCC GV742.42.B855 (ebook)
| DDC 796.092 [B] —dc23
LC record available at https://lccn.loc.gov/2016011271

Printed in the United States of America
1   3   5   7   9   10   8   6   4   2

All photographs courtesy of the author unless otherwise noted.

Set in Adobe Garamond Pro
Designed by Cassandra Garruzzo

To the strong women who have shaped me:
my grandma Lillie; my mom, Carole; my sister, Julie;
my daughters, Natalie and Trudy; and my wife, Michelle,
who has changed my life and shown me how happy I can be.

Contents

Part 1
Can You Hear Me Now?

    Chapter 1
    Uh-Oh   3

Part 2
Jack's Kid

    Chapter 2
    The Adventures of Jasper Pennypucker   23

    Chapter 3
    Now Playing Jack Buck . . . Jack Buck!   39

    Chapter 4
    My First Professional At-Bat   59

    Chapter 5
    Cold Winds   75

Part 3
Thanks, Mr. Murdoch

    Chapter 6
    A Fourth Network   89

    Chapter 7
    Big Jumps   105

    Chapter 8
    Thrills and Chills (and Steroids)   121

Contents

Chapter 9
We Are Blessed   139

Part 4
Good-bye, Dad

    Chapter 10
    The Last Fight   157

Part 5
The Top

    Chapter 11
    This Thing Is Huge   175

    Chapter 12
    Married . . . with Children   189

    Chapter 13
    Buck Rhymes with *Suck*   199

Part 6
The Bottom

    Chapter 14
    Grandstanding   227

    Chapter 15
    The Split   241

    Chapter 16
    Vocal Discord   249

Part 7
Climbing Up Again

    Chapter 17
    Happy Days Are Here Again   269

    Chapter 18
    The Mountaintop   281

    Chapter 19
    So What!   287

Part 1

Can You Hear Me Now?

Chapter 1

Uh-Oh

If you bought this book just to confirm that I am an idiot, I have bad news for you:

You will have to wait a few pages.

Hang in there. You can do it.

In 1994, I started broadcasting NFL games on FOX. I had never broadcast a football game in my life, yet FOX liked me enough to give me a chance.[1]

With live broadcasting, you can prepare as much as you want, and that can make it a little easier, but at some point you just have to do it.

---

1. This is a longer story. We will get to that later.

You never know what situations might arise, and you don't even really know what skills you have. I quickly learned that the good Lord blessed me with one of the most important physical gifts for any sportscaster: a good bladder.

You have probably never thought about this. You probably watch game after game, night after night, eating and drinking without any concern at all for when the guys doing the game get to pee. But we're human. We pee. I don't think Bob Costas and Al Michaels will mind if I tell you this.

I suppose that, like with everything else, each announcer has his own style. Jim Nantz may unzip and say, "Hello, friends!" before firing at the urinal. I mean, I don't know. I haven't asked Jim. But sometimes, finding a chance to pee is harder than you might think, especially in some of the older stadiums, where the bathrooms are not always conveniently located.

You have a limited amount of time during a commercial break to get to your destination and get back. You may have to fight your way through sportswriters, which doesn't make them happy, but they can miss a play and survive. I can't.

Veteran broadcasters understand that in many cases, it is wise to start unzipping before you even arrive. You have to be efficient, or you pay a price later. My father told me: "Never run to a microphone." You don't want to be out of breath. So you have to be able to get to the bathroom fast, catch your breath while you pee, and then calmly walk back into the booth.

In December 1994, my otherwise trusty bladder betrayed me. What can I say? Even the great organs have a bad day at the office once in a while. I was doing a Packers-Falcons game in Milwaukee's County

Stadium. It was a memorable game for a number of reasons. The Packers used to play games in Milwaukee every year, but this was their last home game there. Packers star Sterling Sharpe got injured on what seemed like an innocuous hit, and it ended his career.

At some point during that game, unbeknownst to viewers but *extremely* beknownst to me, I had to pee so bad that I could barely talk. The problem was that, at County Stadium, the football press box was really far from the restroom. You had be Tom Cruise in *Mission: Impossible* to get there in time. There was a catwalk, some kind of pulley-and-ladder system—there might have been a zip line. It was rough.

With a few minutes left in the first half, I was dying. I had to go so bad. But in football, we have a mix of longer and shorter commercial breaks—and the way the game went, all of our commercial breaks at the end of the half were only thirty seconds long. There was no way I could get out of the booth, to the bathroom, and back in thirty seconds. I had a solid forty-second stream in me, plus that long commute. Forget it.

Every time we went to break, I asked, "How long is this one?"

Thirty seconds.

"Jesus!"

At some point I explained my problem to my spotter, Gary. A spotter is the person who helps me during an NFL telecast "spot" who made the catch, who made the tackle, or who blocked a field goal.

I said, "Gary, I've got to go, and I've got to go *now.*"

He was like, "I don't know what to do." This was not a scenario they address in spotter school.[2]

---

2. There is no school for spotters. Announcers often let their buddies be spotters so they can travel with the crew on the network's dime.

I said: "I've *got* to pee. I can't hold this any longer. This is not going to work."

Then I said: "Give me something."

Gary handed me a water bottle. Nice thought, and I appreciate the ingenuity, but no. Not going to work. It's December in Wisconsin, I'm wearing this big parka, and anyway, I can't hit that target. It's too small. Who am I—William Tell?

I knocked the bottle out of Gary's hand. I was beside myself, but I was still calling the game. I said, "All right, next break, I'm going to open this parka. Give me the trash can."

He said, "Really?"

I said, "Hand me the fucking trash can in the next break. If it's not more than thirty seconds, I'm peeing in the trash can."

All right, Joe!

Play stopped. We went to commercial.

I said, "How long is this break?"

Thirty seconds.

I demanded the trash can. There was a young woman in the booth, and I asked her to leave. I put the trash can in front of me, I unzipped, I was ready to go, and . . .

Oh no.

Not now.

Stage fright!

You've got to be *kidding* me. I couldn't pee. I was in the booth, I had my parka open, I didn't know what cameras were on me, and I couldn't bring myself to pee.

I was standing there, unzipped, waiting for the floodgates to open,

6

but they wouldn't. It was like the Heinz commercial when you have to wait for the ketchup to come out of the bottle.

Finally they're counting down: *Ten . . . nine . . .*

And suddenly it's Niagara Falls.

On the first play from scrimmage after the break, Brett Favre took a snap as I kept peeing. People thought broadcasters had their dicks in their hands when they called Favre's games—this time I actually did. Favre looked to his right and threw to Sharpe down the sideline.

"He's going to go for a touchdown!" I said as I kept peeing in the trash can.

Wow, you do kind of sound like an idiot.

What? That's not the story about me being an idiot. That was just a man heeding nature's call while calling a touchdown. We're only getting warmed up here.

The first time I did play-by-play for a major-league team, I was twenty years old. It was 1990. The St. Louis Cardinals were playing at Shea Stadium in New York. My father, the famous broadcaster Jack Buck, let me borrow his private plane to travel to New York, because my own private plane was in the shop, getting its gold-plated cupholders shined.[3]

I was working with an announcer named Al Hrabosky. The Cardinals were playing a doubleheader, because there had been a rainout.

---

3. None of this is true. We weren't rich, and my childhood was not quite what people think it was. We'll get to that soon enough.

We wouldn't be on air for the start of Game 1, because other programming was already scheduled.

The producer said, "We're going to come on the air at six. Whatever is going on, whether we're in the middle of Game 1, between games, or into Game 2, we'll come in wherever we are, recap what's happened to this point."

OK, that sounds great.

Wait. What?

"How do we do that?" I asked.

He said, "Well, we're going to run highlights and you'll just talk through the highlights."

That sounds simple, except that I had no idea how to do it.

They said, "You'll find your way through it."

Well, if the producer says I will find my way through it, then I will. He must know what he's talking about. He's the producer. He produces. That's his job.

So I did what I thought you were supposed to do when you went on TV: I slapped too much makeup on my face. The stage manager, Becky Solomon, was making me up, and it was heavy stuff. I felt like Liza Minnelli.[4] I was in this little booth in Shea Stadium on a scorching-hot summer day. I felt like I was broadcasting in an oven.

At 6:00 P.M., we were in the ninth inning of Game 1. I thought, "Oh, my God. They're going to run a recap of the entire game and I'm going to have to talk through it, and I've never done highlights."

So we came on the air. I said, "Welcome to Shea Stadium! Here we

---

4. I may have looked like her, too.

are in the ninth inning of this doubleheader. We'll look back when we can here and show you how we've gotten to this point."

I went through the highlights, and I was awful. I had no idea how to do them. It was just terrible television. But at least I got through it.

I thought, "The worst is over."

ADVICE FOR YOUNG BROADCASTERS: *Never* tell yourself "The worst is over."

When the game ended, they said, "OK, in between the games, you and Al are going to do a little stand-up."

Stand-up? Like Richard Pryor?

I said, "What does that mean?"

I was told, "We're going to stand up and talk about what you're going to see. In the second segment, Al is going to jog down and interview one of the players on the field, and you'll throw it to him."

Uh, OK.

I did the stand-up, mimicking what I had seen on TV as a boy, and finished with: "When we come back, Al is going to go down to the field and talk to one of the players." We went to commercial. Al ran out of there. Now it was just me. I was sweating. The makeup was running onto my shirt. It was like *Broadcast News*, when Albert Brooks sweats through the newscast.

We were getting ready to go on the air. The producer was in my ear:

"*Five . . . four . . . three . . .*"

I said, "Welcome back to Shea Stadium!"

But I was sweating so much that my earpiece popped out of my ear and fell to the floor.

I should have just said: "I don't know what I'm doing! If you think I only got this job because my father is a beloved broadcaster, you're right! You all win! Now, if you'll excuse me, I'm going to lie down for a bit."

I was talking gibberish, repeating myself, and I was completely on my own. Thankfully, I could throw it to Hrabosky. Or so I thought.

"Now," I said, "let's go down to the field and check in with Al Hrabosky, who has a special guest. Al?"

Al?

Hello?

Al.

Al . . . ?

AL!

The red light in front of me was still on. I knew from watching *The Brady Bunch* that this meant I was still on TV.

Al couldn't find his microphone in the dugout. People working on our broadcast were trying to tell me I couldn't go to him, but I couldn't hear them because my earpiece was on the floor.

Ha-ha, that's so pathetic—

Nope! That's not the story that confirms I'm an idiot either.

That's just a little dose of my own embarrassment for your reading pleasure.

I could tell you about the time I interviewed a player who was standing next to a woman, and I said, "Is that your mom?" and he replied, "No, man, that's my wife."[5] But even *that* is not the story that confirms I am an idiot.

OK. Here we go.

In some ways, I've always felt like I took after my grandfather Joe Lintzenich. He played for the Chicago Bears in the early 1930s and served in the Navy in World War II. He was a loyal husband, a loving father, and a wonderful grandfather.

Also, he was bald.

Yes: bald. Nothing scares a man more than that word. It trumps *audit*, *terrorism*, and *herpes*. Nobody wants to be bald. Go ask any man, "Who would you rather look like: Brad Pitt or Telly Savalas?" Nobody says, "Kojak!"

Bald people just look weird. I'm not worried about offending bald readers here, because half of them are patting the tops of their heads, convincing themselves they aren't *that* bald, and the other half *know* they look weird, which is why they go to great lengths—sometimes ridiculous lengths—to avoid going hairless up top. It doesn't matter how much money they have either. Look at Donald Trump. He is a billionaire, but what he really wants is hair. That's why he goes around the country with that dust mop on his head.

You know what? I understand. I have been so deathly afraid of my retreating follicle troops that, when I was twenty-three, I asked the Cardinals manager—who shall remain nameless, especially to those who

---

5. This actually happened. We will get to that, too.

later watched him manage the Yankees to four world championships—about his hair plugs. I had seen (redacted)'s hairline do its dance move—two steps back and one step forward. I could tell he'd had plugs.

I got the name of his guy, called, and set up an appointment for a postseason sprucing-up in October 1993. Just a little sprinkling the infield, if you will. My first wife, Ann, and I flew from our hometown of St. Louis to New York and stayed at a friend's apartment in Manhattan, and I went in for the operation.

There is a medical term to describe the operation: *fucking barbaric*. I'm not the toughest guy in the world, or even in my broadcast booth, but I'm not a whiner. I have had a broken neck, two back surgeries, dental surgery, and a fractured sternum, and I haven't complained too much. But this hair thing is otherworldly.

It starts by "numbing up" the back of your head with around fifteen shots of Novocain. They keep giving you more shots of Novocain until the pain subsides. Pro tip: The pain NEVER subsides. There is a reason that "get scalp pierced with a needle" is not on anybody's bucket list. And after you get the shots in the back of the head, you get shots in the front of the head. Those hurt even more.

Not long after the third shot goes in, you hear a voice of reason inside your head, asking: "What the fuck is wrong with you? Are you really doing this for HAIR? Who CARES? You don't really need hair! Woody Harrelson and Bruce Willis get work and get laid! They are doing FINE!" But you can't cancel an appointment when you are in the middle of it.

The procedure involves moving hair from the back of your head to the front. It's like if Hannibal Lecter took up gardening.

Moving from the back of the head to the front is the ultimate upgrade for that hair. Those strands go from the Bob Uecker seats to sitting with Mark Cuban—they get a much better view of the action. The total procedure lasts about four hours. I now know how long it takes to go to hell and back.

I felt like I would NEVER feel my head again. It was numb with a dull throb for about five days.

And then . . .

Well, well, well: I had a new, semi-believable hairline. I was pleased. And like any red-blooded American eating a bag of Lay's potato chips, I decided I couldn't stop at just one.

I, Joseph Francis Buck, became a hair-plug addict.

I had a routine to stop my hair follicles from retreating like they were being chased by the IRS. Whenever I had a break in my schedule—usually between the end of football season and the start of baseball—I flew to New York and had the doctor bring them in. You might wonder: Why didn't I save the plane fare and find a hair doctor in St. Louis? Well, we in the Midwest believe we aren't capable of such elaborate procedures. We can make you a burger or build your dining-room table, and we never run out of ranch dressing. But we'll leave the fancy hair operations to people who live near an ocean.

My hairstylist in St. Louis, Sandy, complimented my work. But then said she had *another* client who had had the same procedure in St. Louis, and *that* doctor's work was the best she had ever seen.

Huh? So mine really isn't that great?

You've seen *better*?

I made an appointment with the St. Louis doctor, and I must say: Sandy was right! He *was* better. The guy was brilliant—the end result looked more like a natural hairline. I sat there during my first procedure with him, and instead of hearing a New York–accented cruise director behind me, I just had to listen to four hours of NPR. That was his magic go-juice: NPR. I listened, too, if only to get my mind off the blood running down my neck from the new gash in my "harvest area." I paid attention to *All Things Considered* like I was following directions to disarm a nuclear weapon.

When you are undergoing a medical procedure, there are five words you don't want to hear: "Boy, you are a bleeder!"[6] But that's what he said. And when I had to use the restroom in the middle of the surgery, I found out why.

The nurse was kind enough to put surgical paper up on the mirror, so that while I peed, I wouldn't see what my head looked like mid-procedure. But I am a curious guy. I like to look. I pick things a lot. My nose when I read? *Guilty!* I want to know what's in there. A scab before its time? *Guilty!* Get it off me, even if it bleeds (and now that I know I am a bleeder, you would think I would be smarter than that).

I had not used the restroom during the New York procedure, so I had no opportunity to peek at my head. But in St. Louis, I had my chance. I just barely peeled the corner of the surgical paper back, to peek at my head. Curiosity killed the bald cat, and I almost threw up.

---

6. You just counted to make sure that was five words, didn't you?

I was a bloody mess up top (literally, a bloody mess—I'm not pretending to be British) and I had another two hours to go.

Well, I pissed, I missed, and I tucked it in before I was finished, adding a pattern of dark gray to my light gray sweatpants that would have made Zubaz proud.

I went back in, furious with myself for looking. A couple of hours later, after listening to some NPR host who had clearly taken too much Ambien, I was finished.

A few times over the years, someone said a single sentence to me and changed my life. When I was failing an astronomy class in college, a roommate told me I could drop it. This was a revelation. Drop? What is that? You mean I can walk down to the bursar's office where the class registration is and just *poof*—make it go away?

And then there was the time I was getting a consultation for my seventh hair landscaping when the doctor casually said, "You know, you can get this procedure under a general anesthetic."

Um . . . WHAT?

The needle came off the record, the room brightened, the birds chirped louder, and my nipples tingled. Do you mean I can go to sleep and when I wake up, I will still look like a gashed-up mess, but I will be *finished*? Yes, please!

Procedure number seven went well. I added a few strands to the fun and was recovered in about a week.

I also felt more comfortable when I was on camera. You see, that's the real reason I had hair-replacement surgery:

For TV.

Broadcasting is a brutal, often unfair business, where looks are valued more than skills. I was worried that if I lost my hair, I would lose my job.

OK, that's bullshit. It was vanity. Pure vanity.

I just *told* myself I was doing it for TV.

I am the luckiest man ever, with family and friends and a dream job, and yet I spend an inordinate portion of my life thinking about hair—not just mine, but yours. I admit it doesn't really make sense. If you are losing hair, or have lost it, maybe you understand. I guess I am a jealous man. I cannot stand people who have better hair than I do. That's a problem, since it includes 93 percent of the population.

My lack of hair is accentuated by the size of my head. On social media, people mock my large forehead, but they miss the point. It's not just the fore; my whole head is enormous. It would fit in well in a grocery bin next to the honeydew.

The surgery really is miraculous. People don't look at me and instantly think: "Bald!" That's really all I have accomplished. It's not a Nobel Prize in Physics, but when you drop your astronomy class because you are failing, you learn to shoot lower.

Like many addicts, I was able to manage my addiction for a while without any serious consequences. I felt good about it, and my career kept rolling. In February 2011, Troy Aikman and I called Super Bowl XLV,[7] our third Super Bowl together, and I accomplished my main goal for the night, which was not screwing up. That's the top priority when you do a game of that magnitude: Don't screw it up.

---

7. Forty-five. Not that it matters.

Troy and I had something in common: He wore number 8 with the Cowboys, and I was getting ready for hair-plug operation number eight. By that point, getting new hair was old hat. But I was a ball of stress heading into the operation, and it had nothing to do with my hair.

After nearly two decades of marriage to my former high school girlfriend, I was embroiled in a divorce. It was draining me both emotionally and financially. The night before the procedure, I got into a nasty fight on the phone with my soon-to-be ex-wife. My then-fourteen-year-old daughter, Natalie, got dragged into it. It was not good for anybody.

I am a worrier, and on the morning of the operation, all I could think about was Natalie, who had been dragged into a dumb argument unnecessarily. I just wanted to go in, get a nice nap while the guy with the NPR fetish went to work, and leave with more impressive hair in time for baseball season.

When you are a worrier, you don't enjoy waiting for a doctor. A million thoughts shot through my mind: "What if I don't wake up? What if, when I go to sleep, the doctor puts a couple of clumps where they don't belong?"

To avoid confusion about where the hair goes and where it doesn't, you have one final consultation right before you go under. You sit there and he marks, with a surgical marker, exactly where the new follicles will go. It's like designing a golf course. *We'll put a bunker here, some rough over there, and make sure any putts on your forehead break right to left.*

Well, my operation went well—so well that, with all the hair he was able to move, a four-hour operation turned into a six-and-a-half-hour operation. The doctor said he was "on a roll." Either that, or some show about seventeenth-century jousting was on NPR and he couldn't tear away. The operation went so long that my mom and sister continually checked in with the nurse to make sure I was still alive.

When they wheeled me out, I was totally out of it. My sister looked at my hand. It was swollen to three times its normal size. She was freaked, but the nurse said not to worry—it swelled up because I was lying on it during my snooze.

As it turned out, my hand was fine.

My voice was not.

I finally opened my eyes and looked at my mom and sister in the tiny recovery room. I wanted to make a smart-assed comment, and NOTHING came out. I couldn't talk. I could only whisper.

No matter how hard I tried, I sounded like I was dying.

We called the surgeon's office the next day for assurance that my voice would return.

I wanted to hear: "Don't worry. You will be fine."

What I heard instead: "Well, this happens sometimes after a general anesthetic. It's rare. Your voice should come back soon. Just rest and you'll be fine."

Your voice should come back soon.

Should.

Should?

Should is not a reassuring word to me. I am a hypochondriac. I always expect the worst. If I have a knot in a muscle, I decide it's a tumor. If I tweak my knee, it's a torn ACL. Headache? Aneurysm.

No voice? Broke!

I didn't want to hear that my voice *should* come back soon. We *should* have peace in the Middle East, but do we? I spent the day bombarding my mom with one worst-case scenario after the next. I thought something was really wrong. It wasn't just my hypochondria. My voice didn't feel strained or fatigued. It felt thin, weird, and hopeless—kind of like Lindsay Lohan. I knew my voice wasn't coming back in a matter of hours.

The next morning, I tried a fake opening to a broadcast: "Good afternoon, everyone, and welcome to Major League Baseball on FOX!"

It sounded like "Good afternoon, everyone, and welcome to Major League Baseball on FOX!"

If you were writing a scouting report about me that day, you would have to include: pending divorce, heartbroken kids, legal fees, alimony, gashed head, second-to-last year on a contract, no voice, scared, mad, regretful, and yes, let's just say it:

IDIOT.

People all over the world are suffering through all kinds of maladies, usually through no fault of their own . . . and with elective surgery, something I *did to myself*, I killed my ability to earn a living.

I had one of the best jobs in the world. Did I risk it so I could protect my children? Feed the hungry? House the homeless? No, sir! I did it for HAIR.

Yes, yes: *Joe Buck* does kind of rhyme with *DUMB FUCK*!

I told my bosses, the media, and pretty much everybody else that I had a virus and my voice would come back. I was too scared and embarrassed to tell them the truth. But I'm doing it now.

The voice that I had worked so hard to develop, command, and protect was gone. I felt like my identity vanished with it. From the time I was eight years old, I considered only one career: sportscaster. I wondered if I had blown it forever.

Part 2

Jack's Kid

Chapter 2

The Adventures of Jasper Pennypucker

Imagine the prototypical American childhood, with games of catch on the front lawn and the father tucking his son into bed every night.

Mine was much cooler than that.

What can I say? I was lucky. Around the time I was born, my dad's broadcasting career really began to take off. The Cardinals fired their lead broadcaster, Harry Caray, making my father the undisputed Voice of the Cardinals on the radio. He also did NFL games for CBS-TV and radio for many years.

We got along so well. When I was three years old, he would let me sit in his office while he did radio interviews on the phone, as long as I stayed quiet. I *always* stayed quiet. I could tell when his voice got deeper and more precise that he was doing an interview and not just talking to a friend on the phone. I was as happy as I could be, just sitting there watching him. I could not think of anything better than being with him.

I was too worried about consequences to ever get into real trouble. He was too consumed by fun to worry about disciplining me. He mostly left that to my mom. Truthfully, even though he was forty-four when I was born, he was more like my best friend than my dad.

When I was little, he came up with a nickname for me: Jasper Pennypucker.[8] But after that, he always called me Buck. He took me everywhere.

Some kids go to summer camp. I did that and I hated it. So instead, I went to Cardinals baseball games. When I was four, the Cardinals catcher saw this little guy with an enormous head bounding through the clubhouse, acting like he lived there, and he asked, "Who *is* this kid?"

Somebody said, "Oh, that's Jack's kid. That's Joe."

That was the first time I met Tim McCarver.

When I was three or four, I got excited about something at a Cardinals game, which was only a problem because (a) I knocked over a Coke, (b) I was in the press box, not in the stands, and (c) the Coke landed on my father and his radio partner while they were on the air. They didn't know what happened. They thought somebody came in and just threw something down on them.

---

8. I look forward to this book coming out and seeing signs in the crowd at a ball game that read "EAT SHIT, JASPER PENNYPUCKER!" Come on, America. Don't disappoint me.

They turned around in the middle of the broadcast and looked at me. I burst out crying, thinking I'd just ruined everything for everybody. But they kept doing the game.

All I wanted, as long as I can remember, was to be him. When he was home, we'd eat dinner, go downstairs, and play pool against each other. He treated me like his buddy.

At other times, we would get in the car and drive to this other house in town. We would walk up to the front door, and when it opened, there would be a woman and some older kids inside.

They were my dad's first family.

We were there to drop off a check for alimony and child support.

I was scared to death. Everybody there gave me the distinct, uncomfortable feeling that I wasn't wanted. I didn't understand why at the time, but I represented something painful in their lives.

When my parents met, my mom was a Broadway actress and my dad was a married man. My mom's name was Carole Lintzenich (stage name: Carole Lindsay), and she was doing a musical with a touring company in her hometown of St. Louis. He was talking to her on a pay phone outside of the Chase Park Plaza hotel, home to one of the hottest bars in St. Louis in the sixties, when she told him she was pregnant.

"I feel like my knees are melting into the pavement," he said.

He already had six children with his wife, Alyce. He left her—and, by extension, them—for my mom. They got married in March 1969. One month later, she gave birth to a boy with a large head who cried a lot, probably because he was born bald.

That was me, obviously.

To use the indelicate term of those times: I was a bastard child.

It was 1969. The public did not talk about the sex lives of famous people like they do today.[9] So there was no major scandal or significant public fallout. But there were some deep wounds, and some tense moments for me and my sister, Julie, who was born three years after me.

The memory of helping deliver those alimony checks is still painful. To this day, I don't know why my dad made me go with him. Maybe he thought it would force everybody to be civil. He was nonconfrontational to the point of being avoidant. My presence gave him a better chance of getting out of there without a fight.

I didn't really interact with my half siblings often—just enough to make me feel incredibly uncomfortable. My dad would put us all on KMOX, the fifty-thousand-watt radio station where he worked, on Christmas morning. Sometimes we did the show from my house— entertaining the people of St. Louis instead of wondering what Santa brought down the chimney. When I was around twelve, I played the trumpet on the KMOX show in the studio. I felt like my half siblings were glaring at me. I was fat and I sucked at the trumpet anyway, and now I was playing "What Child Is This?" for people thinking, "Yeah, Dad, what child is *that*?" I didn't want to play—not on the radio, and especially not for them. What a great Christmas! *Happy birthday, Jesus! Can you take me now? Or take them?* I was not mad at my father, but I was embarrassed at having to perform in front of these people.

My half brother Danny was a really good local football player and

---

9. What did they do with all that free time?

a big, strong guy, and one day at his house, he said, "Come here, Joe, let's go dive into the pool." It was a statement, not a question.

Danny put me on his shoulders. I was this dopey fat kid. He dove in, which made me smack the water. It took everything I had in me to not cry. But it hurt. It hurt on a lot of levels, but I mean, it *physically* hurt. I got out of the pool, and my skin was red. I'm sure my face was red with embarrassment, too.

I went inside, and my father's ex-wife was cooking hot dogs.

She said, "Do you want a hot dog?"

I said, "Yeah, that would be great."

And she said, "What do you like on it?"

I said, "I just like ketchup. The only thing I don't like is mustard."

She gave me a hot dog with mustard all over it. That's a little thing, but I remember it like it was yesterday. I smiled and ate every bite of that fucking hot dog. But I felt miserable. And that stuff was always gurgling under the surface whenever I saw them. There was this undercurrent of deep-seated animosity, and I understand where it started now, but I didn't get it then. To me, my dad was the greatest guy in the world.

With the tension with my dad's ex-wife and older kids hovering, he bought my mom a bracelet with two words on it: *So What!*

I'm sure my dad didn't have a ton of money to spend on jewelry. When he gave her that bracelet, I think it hit home with my mom: So what if they're not nice to you? If people are talking about us in St. Louis, so what? It doesn't matter.

He wanted us to enjoy our lives, and we did. He felt he had missed too much time with his older kids because he was working, and he vowed not to make that mistake again. He was still on the road a lot, but he took me with him when he could—to make up for at least *some* of the time we missed.

So much of the fun happened around ballparks. I walked to the home radio booth at Busch Stadium so often, I could do it with my eyes closed. To this day, I can do that walk in my mind: into the press box, turn right, and go into the first door on the left. That was the KMOX radio booth. It was two-tiered. In the back of the booth were two counters with two chairs at each spot. That was where guests sat. You could often find my dad's best friend, Joe Arndt, there. If my dad was interviewing anybody on the air, they sat in one of those chairs until it was time to do the interview.

In the front of the booth, four or five steps away, there were four seats. From left to right as you faced the field, you would see:

- A radio engineer, who would turn mics on for each half inning, time the commercial breaks, and keep track of the out-of-town scoreboard.
- My father.
- His broadcast partner, Mike Shannon.
- A fourth seat, with half a pair of canned headphones. There was no microphone—just a single earpiece you could hold up and listen to the broadcast.[10] That's where I would sit for most of the games.

---

10. It was like a prehistoric version of Beats by Dre.

I loved that seat. When I listened to that little earphone, I could hear the mix of the broadcast: the announcers mixed with the crowd mixed with the crack of the bat. It was like listening to the radio right there while they did it. I could hear the subtleties and nuance of the broadcast, and I could watch them as they did it.

I learned the mechanics of how they did their job. A baseball radio broadcast is not like an orchestra. There is no conductor. My dad didn't point to Mike as if to say, "OK, now it's your turn." They signaled that they had something to say with a subtle shift in a chair or a lean into the microphones.

I would watch my dad say, "At the end of the fifth, the score is Cardinals 4, Pirates 2," and control when they went into a commercial break. I saw the bullshit between innings, my dad and Mike looking through binoculars at some woman in the seats. I realized it was not a stiff existence. They were having a blast.

Then I would see the producer, Tom Barton, holding his stopwatch and counting down so they would know when they were back on the air: "15 . . . 10 . . . 5 . . . you got it!"

And I would watch a play unfold live and hear my dad describe it. "What a play to his right!" he would say, as Ozzie Smith robbed somebody of a single. I would think about how I would call it. I was getting father-son bonding time and professional training simultaneously every night of every summer.

As I got older, Butch Yatkeman, the clubhouse guy, let me be a batboy for the team. Butch was this little guy who was the Cardinals equipment manager forever. That's when I got to know a lot of the players.

Butch tried to find me uniform pants, but it wasn't easy. The typical batboy uniform was built for a little kid, and I got my clothes from the "husky" section at Sears.[11] I took one look at the batboy pants and thought, "I'm not fitting into those." I ended up wearing some player's pants, which was so embarrassing.

Once we got that humiliation out of the way, we moved on to another.

"God, this hat doesn't fit you either," Butch said, and he was right. Even then, my head was enormous.

Being around those players, though, and being in that atmosphere as a little kid was awesome—even though I didn't fully appreciate it. It was just part of my life. Sometimes I'd run around and shag fly balls in the outfield before games. I have a picture of me playing catch with Dave Rader, the Cardinals catcher. I was eight years old.

During a game in San Francisco's Candlestick Park when I was thirteen, a player gave me chewing tobacco. I put it in my mouth and let it settle in for a minute. I thought I was cool. Then I got light-headed and threw up. I zigzagged my way out of there to pick up bats like I was trying to escape an alligator, while the players roared with laughter on the bench.

One of my best friends at the time was Jon Simmons, whose father, Ted, was an eight-time Major League All-Star. Sometimes, while our dads were working—mine in the broadcast booth, Jon's in the batter's

---

11. It's not like I was circus-fat. But I was chubby.

box—we would be downstairs at Busch Stadium, throwing tennis balls at each other or playing stickball.

As much fun as I had at home games, road trips were even better. Every city was like an amusement park I would get to explore. When the Cardinals played in Los Angeles, my dad and I would leave the team after the series and fly home ourselves. That way, we could stop in Las Vegas. We stayed at the Dunes Hotel because he had a friend there who comped him.

My dad grew up during the Depression. He loved having some "walking-around money," as he called it, and he loved gambling. So we would get to the Dunes and eat. Then he would hand me a ten- or twenty-dollar bill and say, "Here, go to the arcade. I'm going to go roll craps. I'll see you in the morning."

I'd go play Donkey Kong, Pac-Man, and Space Invaders until I ran out of money. Then I would go up to the room. I wouldn't see my father 'til he opened the door at 7:00 A.M. to pick me up and go to the airport. He never went to bed. He gambled all night.

I remember one time he had a wad of hundreds, and I'd never seen him so happy. Another time he had nothing. He said, "Well, we worked for free this week, Buck. Don't tell your mother. Let's go."

My dad loved baseball and loved the Cardinals, but mostly, he loved excitement. He loved being part of a scene. When celebrities came through St. Louis, they invariably wanted to go to a ball game. The Cardinals got them in, and they ended up in the broadcast booth. I met Frank Sinatra, Billy Crystal, Bill Murray, and Olympic athletes from various sports. Later, St. Louis native John Goodman came by a lot.

Our house was kind of a communal place. My dad loved to entertain. Pro athletes would come by our house to play poker. They would drink and smoke, and I'd sit on my father's lap and throw chips in for him. I didn't understand poker then, and I still don't. But I loved being around it.

My parents attended parties where people sang and played piano, and not just any people. They were friends with Tony Bennett, and the comedian Norm Crosby, and Donald O'Connor, an actor who appeared in *Singin' in the Rain*. They had the greatest time.

My dad was the star of the family, but my mom was the soul. She is the definition of a shirt-off-her-back person who has time for everyone—a religious woman who wishes her son would go to church more. She gets great strength from reading and studying the Bible; she lives by it better than anyone I know. Yes, I know this sounds strange, considering my father was married when they met. But she became more religious during my childhood, and I've watched her give all she can give to person after person. She is the best example my children can have for how to live a life and do what's right and help those who need it.

It was not a fluke, in my opinion, that my dad's career took off when they got married. She was a huge part of his success. She was his guide and compass—and sometimes his joke writer. She either wrote or "punched up" some of his best banquet lines—they would sit in our kitchen together and work, like a comedy team.

And sometimes, she delivered the jokes herself. I remember a charity roast for my dad in the early eighties. My mom was one of the roasters. My half siblings were there.

My mom stepped to the microphone and said, "Why should we roast Jack Buck, when he gets burned every month when he writes his alimony check?" My dad did a spit take on the dais. I saw it on TV and couldn't believe what I had just heard. Considering the audience, it took some guts for her to say it. I loved it. My sister, Julie, loved it. I think even my father loved it. It was a claw back at people who were not nice to her.

When I was ten, my parents took Julie and me to New York. Julie was seven. We were staying at the Grand Hyatt. My dad was not going to let his kids get in the way of his night on the town with his wife. Before he and my mom went to dinner, he gave me a fifty-dollar bill and said, "There's a McDonald's a couple blocks up and across the street. Take your sister to dinner there, and come back to the room and watch TV and go to bed."

It's hard for me to imagine leaving two preteen kids on their own for a night in New York. But it was the 1970s, and societal concepts of child safety were different. Most parents seemed to think that if their kids wanted to play with fire, it was OK as long as it was a *small* fire.

As Julie and I walked toward McDonald's, we saw a crowd. In the middle, a guy was moving three shells around. There was a pea under one of the shells, and as he moved the shells, you had to keep track of the pea.

I stood in the back of the crowd. I'm sure the guy saw me immediately. I don't know what kind of school you have to go to to be a street hustler, but I bet there is an entry-level class on how to pull a ten-year-old out of a crowd.

The hustler kept moving shells numbers one and two. But he appeared to leave shell number three untouched.

Like *completely* untouched.

I mean, there was *no way* the pea could end up under shell number three.

Then he said to another guy in the crowd, "You, sir. Which one is it under?"

The guy in the crowd pointed to shell number one. The hustler picked it up. There was no pea. He took the money. Now only shells numbers two and three were left. And as we previously established, the hustler had not even touched shell number three! There was *no way* the pea could be under shell number three.

So the hustler turned to me: "Hey, young man. I'll match whatever money you got in your pocket if you can tell me where the pea is under one of these two shells."

My parents raised me well. I knew that any game had to be played honestly. So I told him the truth:

"I only have a fifty."

I figured there was no way this poor guy had fifty dollars on him, and I wanted to give him a chance to walk away before I embarrassed him. But he just said, "That's fine. Which one's it under?"

I pointed to the obvious answer: shell number two. He flipped it over. There was nothing there. Then he flipped over shell number three—and there was the pea! A *stunning* development!

He ripped the fifty out of my hand. I looked at my sister. *Good-bye, Big Mac! We hardly knew ye.* Julie and I went back to the hotel and ordered room service.

When I woke up the next morning, my dad wanted to know two things: Why was there a room-service tray outside our door? And where was the change from his fifty-dollar bill?

So I told him what happened. Some parents would have been furious, but he loved a good story. He thought it was hilarious. He told every Cardinals player: *Listen to how fucking dumb my kid is. He gets sucked into a shell game and tells the guy, "I've only got a fifty!"* The players were killing me, just killing me.

By the time I was a teenager, the games were an incredibly fun part of the day, but not the only fun part. I remember one off day in Los Angeles when we went to the beach in the morning with Mike Shannon, my dad's broadcast partner, and Mike's son, Danny. Then we went to Hollywood Park and caught five or six races. That night we went to Dodger Stadium in time for the Dodgers and Cardinals game.

It was a little more fun than running errands and playing Atari.

At the end of the night, we went back to the hotel and there was this carpet with all these different squares. Mike Shannon said, "Why don't you boys count how many squares there are between here and the far wall?" We sat there and counted deliberately: *one, two, three, four . . .*

When we were finished counting, we turned around. Mike and my dad were gone.

They were right around the corner, laughing.

At least I didn't lose fifty dollars *that* time.

For most of my childhood, the Cardinals were not very good. Or at least, they were never *great*. They played in the 1968 World Series a few months before I was born, but they didn't make the playoffs again until 1982.

My dad and Mike Shannon were doing the Cardinals' World Series games on the radio, and they moved from their regular booth to one in the football press box, down the right-field line, because the network TV people bumped them out of their regular prime location. I was in the booth with them. Tug McGraw, the longtime Mets and Phillies pitcher, was there, too. He was a friend of my dad's. I don't know how or why they became friends. My father was just a friend magnet.

The World Series obviously felt a lot different from a June game in Pittsburgh. My father and Mike were excited. When the Cardinals won Game 7, my dad said, "That's a World Series winner for the Cardinals!" He watched fans rush the field, swarming Monsanto's famous AstroTurf, where mounted police were waiting, and said, "Those fans won't be there for long." He meant they would be arrested. He was wrong. Pretty soon it was mayhem, with fans all over the field. There were not enough handcuffs in St. Louis to arrest everybody who rushed the field that night.

I had turned thirteen that year. Thirteen years old is right around the peak of fandom for most sports fans—at that age, you understand the games and you have a little perspective, but not *too* much perspective. But it was different for me than for all the other kids out there. I was excited the Cardinals won, but it was a different kind of excited from what most thirteen-year-old Cardinals fans felt. The Cardinals weren't really heroes to me. They weren't these unreachable, untouchable guys. I had already peeked behind the curtain.

For example: When Whitey Herzog was hired to be the Cardinals manager, in the middle of the 1980 season, I watched my dad interview him in the radio booth the day he was hired. Whitey was louder than a typical radio guest, and he kind of pulled me down the steps at one point.

I asked my dad afterward, "Was he drunk?" He said yes.

Pitcher Dave LaPoint once playfully punched me in the shoulder, as a one-of-the-guys kind of teasing, but it hurt so bad that tears streamed down my face. He felt awful. First baseman Keith Hernandez liked my father, so he liked me. Second baseman Tommy Herr would hire my sister, Julie, as his babysitter a few years later.

On Ozzie Smith's first day in St. Louis, he came to our house and I played catch with him. I was probably the first kid in St. Louis to learn Ozzie was such a magician with his glove. He said, "Just throw it to my glove." He was able to make the ball ricochet from his glove into his bare hand, without moving either one of them. It was unbelievable.

Seeing the players every day, joking before and after games, made me realize that people in sports do not view the games the same way that fans do. When I was little, I woke up in a good mood if the Cardinals won the night before and was depressed if they lost. But to players,

baseball was a job. They did their best, but they understood that sometimes they would have a bad day at the office.

They could even laugh about it. I remember the great Cardinals
closer Lee Smith giving up a game-winning home run one day. On the
plane ride that night, he gathered some teammates together and said,
"I threw a slider . . . one side of the ball said 'hit me,' and the other
one said 'hard!'" They laughed. If they could handle a loss, why would
I lose sleep over it?

So at a fairly young age, I realized that while I loved sports, I was
not the same kind of fan that my friends were. I wasn't emotionally
invested in teams winning or losing—I just enjoyed being around
them. To this day, people ask me: Is it hard not to be a fan on the air?
It's not hard. The truth is, I lost the "fan" part of me before I was a
professional broadcaster.[12]

---

12. When Bryce Harper steps into the batter's box and thinks, "I hope Joe Buck has a
great game today," I will start cheering for him, too.

Chapter 3

Now Playing Jack Buck . . . Jack Buck!

Every year, my mom and I had a routine. I would sign up for Little League baseball, and she would freak out. She thought it was too dangerous. Like I was going to get killed by a batted ball or something.

She'd say, "Hardball?" *No, Mom, they replaced them with Wiffle balls this year.* It became our little joke. And it's kind of funny to think that my dad spent most of the year telling the masses about this wonderful game of baseball, and my mom didn't even want me to play. If they ever hold a contest for the most overprotective, worried mother of all time, she should win.

I almost did get killed by a batted ball once, but I was in the stands when it happened. My family was in Cincinnati for a Cardinals road trip, and when we got to Riverfront, I begged my mom to buy me a Cardinals batting helmet. She didn't want to do it. She pointed out that I had roughly seven hundred of them at home and didn't need another. I argued that I wasn't home, and I wanted one, so *please, Mom, please, please, please!* She relented and bought me one.

We sat in our seats behind the third-base dugout. Early in the game, my mom told me to duck my head if a ball came toward us. Sure enough, the Reds' Pete Rose came up to bat left-handed and slapped a foul ball right at us. I ducked and it hit my batting helmet, leaving a mark. The ball landed in the guy's lap behind me.

My dad was doing the game on the radio. He said, "Oh, a dangerous foul ball in the seats," and he looked through his binoculars and saw my mom and me. He was terrified.

I was fine, though. That cheap batting helmet might have saved me. I kept the helmet for years, but not the ball—the man sitting behind us refused to give it to me.[13]

I guess it was appropriate that my father was working and my mother was sitting next to me when that happened. My mom was our confidant. She was our disciplinarian. She was the one who made everything OK. She supported us completely, even if it meant we might get hit in the head.

She gave up her career when she got pregnant with me, and she never looked back. She would sing at parties, but that was it. She never tried to restart her career. She was never bitter, never upset. She just

---

13. What a dick.

was a great wife and a great mom who filled all the holes that were there because my dad was gone so much.

Because I was a good high school baseball player, people made the connection to my father. But whatever athletic ability I have (or had), I got from my mom's side. She was a physical education major at Washington University in St. Louis. Her father played for the Bears. Her brother was a great high school athlete.

My dad wasn't a great athlete. He was kind of awkward. He loved to play golf, but he never got good at it. My mom is the one who taught me how to play baseball, even though she didn't want me to play. Our house shared a driveway with the house next door, and there was this little grassy area in the middle of it, and my mom taught me how to throw a baseball and hit a baseball there. We would play catch, and she would sling it to me sidearm, so that was how I threw, too. Eventually, I was playing catch with Major Leaguers when I was hanging around Busch Stadium.

I never really played catch with my dad. We'd play on the beach in spring training. But I was so deathly afraid of overthrowing him because then he'd have to go chase it down the beach, and I didn't want to make him do that.

One time we had Bruce Bochy over to our house—he was a catcher in the National League, and even though he never played for the Cardinals, he and my dad were friends. My father said, "You've got to see my wife punt a football. She can punt a football over this house." That was true. He was in awe of my mom's ability to punt.

Then my dad said, "You know, I used to kick a little bit." He spun the ball to get it in the right position, then tried to kick it. It hit the side of his foot and he drilled Bochy right in the nuts. He was rolling around on the ground. My dad was mortified. He should have left the punting to my mom.

The first time I saw my dad on TV, I cried. I thought he was stuck in there.[14] Then I got used to it—so used to it, in fact, that I assumed everybody else's father was often in a TV, too.

At times, it seemed like my life would have been easier if everybody else's father *was* in the TV. Then they would have left mine alone. But all of my friends thought it was cool that they knew Jack Buck. They remember stories about him that I've long since forgotten. To me, it was just something my dad said, but to them, it came out of the mouth of Jack Buck.

I came to understand that "Jack Buck" was not just his name. It was the part he played for most of his adult life. He was the Cardinals' radio play-by-play announcer when that meant even more than it does today. For much of his career, there was no cable TV. A lot of Cardinals games weren't even televised. Entertainment options were limited. If you lived in St. Louis, Jack Buck was the sound track of your summers.

Playing the part of Jack Buck meant that when somebody asked you to speak at a function, you spoke. It didn't matter if it was the Kiwanis club, a high school awards banquet, or a luncheon for local police. He would speak at three or four events a week in the off-season.

I know I'm biased, but thousands of St. Louisans will tell you he

---

14. Clearly, I was not a candidate for Baby Mensa.

was the best after-dinner speaker they ever heard in their lives. There was nobody you'd rather listen to between the rubber chicken and dry chocolate cake.

He would tell the crowd he was "a proud father of eight children—all boys, except for five." When people applauded, he would say, "Don't applaud. It took me a total of forty minutes to make that happen—and that includes the conversation."

I think he enjoyed making people laugh during those speeches as much as he enjoyed broadcasting games. Maybe more. It was a chance for him to show more of his personality, more of his talent.

I think that explains why, at the height of his Cardinals career, he quit.

The year was 1975. He left the Cardinals for a chance to host a new NBC studio highlight show from New York called *Grandstand*. NBC wanted *Grandstand* to be a sports wraparound show to compete with ABC's *Wide World of Sports*. My dad would get to stretch creative muscles he never used during a baseball game.

I was six at the time. When the Cardinals announced over the Busch Stadium loudspeakers that my dad was leaving the team, I was in the booth with him. The fans stood and applauded. My dad looked out at the crowd and gave a six-shooter salute back, then turned away and wept.

I can still see him weeping. When you're a little boy and you see your father cry, you don't forget it.

Back then, I didn't understand why he would leave a job he loved, or why he would be willing to commute (and possibly move) to New York when we loved St. Louis so much. But now I see why he did it. I'm sure money was a factor, but I think he also wanted to let people know he was more than a play-by-play announcer. Being part of a national TV studio show was a huge professional opportunity.

He had an innate sense of timing and a wicked, cutting sense of humor. He also had a worldview that went beyond sports. I always read the sports section of the newspaper first. He started with the front section, which I use to start fires. He had a sense of history and read biographies. I can't even spell *biographies* without spell-check.

He was enamored of the human condition and was a terrific interviewer—always listening to an answer, because it usually led to his next question. If there were one person in an otherwise empty bar, he would sit next to that person and begin an interrogation. He had an incredible thirst to learn about people, whether it was Andrew Jackson or Reggie Jackson.

Grandstand was a ratings and critical disappointment. I don't remember the show at all, but from what I've heard, it was a mess. It did launch somebody's career as a national TV star, but that somebody was not Jack Buck. It was his cohost, a young man named Bryant Gumbel, who became one of the faces of NBC.

I have been told that the banter between my dad and Bryant during breaks was more interesting than what they said on the air. I've also heard that some of my dad's funniest lines during those breaks magically came out of Bryant's mouth once the red light went on. That could be bullshit—Buck family revisionism—but anyway, it was not the biggest issue.

Gumbel is terrific at television. I remember meeting him when I was a kid, and I could tell, even then, that he was the alpha in the situation. He was the young, brash upstart, and he was great. He just upstaged my father. My dad had done radio for so long and so well, and he never quite figured out how to be great on TV.

In 1976, he came home from a trip to New York on a Sunday night and told my mom, "They tied a can to me." I had never heard that before, but I soon learned what it meant. He had been fired.

He was disappointed, of course. But the Cardinals gladly took him back, and he quickly resumed his career as one of the most popular men in town.

Almost everybody in St. Louis seemed to think of my dad as family. I had to share him with the city. It could be hard to differentiate between the public role of Jack Buck and the private man who helped raise me.

In high school, I was scared to drink a beer at a party because I didn't want it to reflect poorly on him. When we went out to dinner, it felt like we were meeting up with everybody in St. Louis. It was no secret that our family meeting place was Cunetto House of Pasta, or as everybody calls it, Cunetto's. It's on a hill not far from my dad's first home when he moved to St. Louis. Yogi Berra and Joe Garagiola were from the same neighborhood. My dad knew the Cunetto brothers, Vince and Joe, when they ran a pharmacy. The brothers opened a restaurant in 1974. I was five years old.

One morning, my father mentioned it on a radio call-in show he was hosting: *"I had the best meal last night at this great new restaurant, Cunetto's. . . ."* From that night on, there was a line out the door to get in the place.

So they always loved my dad, and he wasn't lying: He really did love that place. And every time we had a big family dinner, we did it at Cunetto's. We never said, "OK, let's really do something special," or "Let's find the nicest restaurant in town," or "Let's try this new, hot place," or "Isn't anybody sick of pasta? We've been eating it for thirteen years!"

We always went to Cunetto's. There really wasn't any other place on our list. I don't know if they gave my dad a discount, or if he paid full price. I never asked. But that was where we went.

And when we got there, people saw my father and acted like he was a member of their family. He never shooed them away. It didn't matter who they were, or where we were sitting, or if we were in the middle of dinner. If people walked to our table, he would talk to them. Sometimes he'd even pull out a chair.

Some guy would say, "Hey, Jack, I met you at a Kiwanis club back in '68."

I'd think, "Yeah, whatever."

And my dad would say, "Hey, didn't you have a mom who was a chef?"

And the guy would say, "Yes!"

His memory for that kind of stuff was astonishing. I see why everybody in St. Louis loved him. But I loved him more. And as a boy, I thought: "He is *my* dad, not theirs." I felt like we were getting intruded upon. I would think, "Come on. I've been waiting for him to get home for two weeks." We didn't have cell phones then. It's not like he was checking in every minute, calling and texting us. Long-distance calls from a hotel room were expensive. When he was gone, he was *gone.* His time at home was valuable to me. I didn't want to share him with strangers. But I had no choice. He was always throwing out the welcome mat.

This is something I should probably discuss with a psychologist, but I'm going to share it with readers instead.[15] Anyway, I think my father was such a people person—and such a people *pleaser,* really—that it took some of the uniqueness away from Julie's and my relationship with him. He was available to everybody. It was like we shared him with the entire city. And for my half brothers and half sisters, that was really the case. They just never got to spend the time with him that I did.

In other cities, my dad was probably just another announcer. In St. Louis, he was this odd mix of royalty and politician—people revered him, and he was always happy to shake a few hands.

If you are an American of my generation, you probably remember a TV show called *Lifestyles of the Rich and Famous.* It was hosted by this British guy named Robin Leach, who would go around the world showing you that rich and famous people had enormous, diamond-studded rooms where they would have servants wax their toe hairs. It was like an early version of *MTV Cribs.* As I learned, my dad would have been half-qualified for Leach's show:

He was famous. But he wasn't rich.

And he was always *very* conscious of that.

---

15. Some of you are probably psychologists. The rest of you can fake it.

A lot of times, when we went to Cunetto's, he would take out a black Bic felt-tip pen and calculate his net worth. He would write on a napkin that would tear a bit when he wrote on it. And when he did it, he counted *everything:* his retirement plan, his bank account, equity in his house, the value of his car, and if he had a contract that he had signed, money he hadn't even been paid yet—everything but the furniture in our house. Then he'd subtract the taxes he owed.

He knew exactly where his pennies were. I think that's probably natural coming from a kid who grew up in the Depression and had nothing, and all of a sudden had found . . . not riches, but something. He always wanted to make sure he had enough money. He never said no to any work. He just did it.

He was obsessed with having a net worth of $1 million. It was weird, because he was really terrible with money in many ways. He never stood up for himself and asked for raises. He didn't really look into retirement accounts and other ways he could have improved his financial situation. He left a lot of money on the table in negotiations because he didn't hire an aggressive, high-powered agent. (Some of those nights in Vegas did not help his bottom line either.)

But that was his life's goal, getting to the other side of that second comma: $1,000,000. So he would pull out that felt-tip pen in Cunetto's, and I would think: "We're doing this *again*? We just did this a few months ago." But if something else came in—a new broadcasting gig, or a contract to do Anheuser-Busch commercials, anything that added to his income—he would start a new tally.

Eventually, my sister and I would get up and walk around the parking lot while he calculated his net worth. He'd stay with my mom and do the math. Julie and I would be walking around in the middle of a hill in a slanted parking lot, dodging death. When we got back to the table, we would often find other people standing there, ready to chat with my dad for a few more minutes.

My dad had sent all his older kids to public school, with no reservations. He was more than happy with the public schools in little Ladue, Missouri. But my mom had gone to John Burroughs, a private school, and she wanted me to go to private school. She won the vote, 1–0.

I started going to Country Day in fifth grade. Country Day was a school for rich kids. Kids who would go on to own the Cardinals or run businesses in St. Louis went to Country Day. People who spent their weekends at country clubs went to Country Day.

We were not rich. My father was writing checks from a much smaller bank account than the other parents. We certainly never wanted for anything, but he felt real financial pressure, with a divorce and a lot of kids to support. He was constantly scrambling, taking every job he could get—Cardinals radio, NFL football on CBS, *Monday Night Football* on the radio, sports director at KMOX, a morning call-in show at KMOX, call-in shows at night.

I don't know where he found the energy to do so many different jobs. But add them all together and he could afford to send me to private school . . . barely. I think he was paying five grand a year back then for me to go, and it was stressful for him. With every passing year, as tuition went up, he got more stressed.

Thankfully for him, I paid him back getting straight As.

Wait, did I say As? I meant Bs.

I got Bs because getting Bs was easy. I never really tried to get As, and never was lazy enough to get many Cs.

Country Day was a little prep school—we had sixty-some boys in my graduating class, and the majority of us had been together since fifth grade. It was the same cliques, the same groups the whole way. I was never in the "cool" group, but I had friends because I was pretty athletic and I could be funny. Those are still some of my best friends.

We had all male teachers, and if you messed up, some of them would paddle you, rap your knuckles, or throw erasers at you. These days, if a teacher did that, he would get sent to Guantanamo Bay and CNN would cover it. But back then we accepted it as part of life.

Even though we didn't have many students, our sports teams were usually pretty good. In my class (the class of '87) we had guys on our football team who went to Division I college football programs, like my friend Turner Baur, who played at Stanford and got drafted by the Patriots. We had a guy who went to Air Force and a few who played in the Ivy League.

I played football as well. I pitched for the baseball team, so you would think that I could have played quarterback, but I had two problems that kept me from playing quarterback. In order, my problems were:

1. Fat.
2. Slow.

You know where they put the fat, slow guys: on the line. I played on the C team as a freshman, I played on the B team sophomore year, and then by my junior year, I was part of the varsity team. I was not an integral part, in the sense of "helping" the team "win," but they did not take my uniform away. I joked later that I would eat onions so I would have the worst possible breath, then stand next to the coach and keep asking him when I was going in. And when I was a junior, even that didn't work.

But going into my senior year, I was a starter at both offensive and defensive tackle. Then, in one of our last contact practices leading up to the opening game of my senior year, I was running in to make a tackle, and I ended up meeting our running back, Mike Mayweather, helmet to helmet.[16]

The thing about "helmet-to-helmet" hits is that there are heads inside those helmets. I was in real pain. I got knocked down and it took ten seconds for me to get feeling back in my body and get up again.

At that point, in the great tradition of high school football coaches, our coaches started riding me: "Finally you make a great hit, and now you're hurt!" There is a reason high school football coaches do not work for Hallmark in their spare time. I went to the sideline for a minute to regain my senses.

I knew something wasn't right. But I'm a pleaser, and I wanted to make my coaches happy. So I started both ways in that first game, and played the whole way. Then the next Monday rolled around and I was sore beyond belief. My neck was killing me. I finally told my coach I needed to see a teammate's dad who was a doctor. He begrudgingly agreed.

The doctor came out of his office and said, "You're not going to

---

16. Mayweather would go on to set rushing records at Army.

believe this, but your neck is broken." I had a clean fracture at C6, for those scoring on your spinal charts at home. He told me I was done playing football and asked me to wear a neck collar. I politely declined the neck collar. I was eighteen and already insecure enough. I didn't need to walk around the hallways at Country Day looking like a chubby dog with a cone around my neck.

I told my head coach my neck was broken. He paused, blew his whistle, and resumed practice. I wanted to say, "Hello? Did you hear me? I played a game with a broken neck!"

My football "career," such as it was, was over. But I could still play baseball. I was a pretty good pitcher—I even had scouts watch me occasionally. My dad was always fairly low-key at my games. He tried to hide in the background so nobody could see he was there. But they always knew. He was older than the other parents, and one of the most recognizable guys in St. Louis.

One time I was pitching for Country Day as a junior, and my dad took a red-eye flight just to be there. He pulled up by the little baseball field at Country Day in his Lincoln Mark VI, dust flying behind it, as we were warming up.

He went out to talk to me before the game, to wish me luck. I told him my arm was killing me. He advised me to just throw fastballs and changeups, and stay away from curveballs and sliders. When the game started, I lost control of the very first pitch, a fastball, and hit Brentwood High School's tiny leadoff batter squarely in the helmet. Everybody looked at my father like he had told me to drill the first hitter. He put his hands up, as if to say, "Hey, I didn't tell him to do that!"

I thought I might get a baseball scholarship to Duke—the coach said he might have room on the team if I could get admitted. But then he didn't have any scholarships, and I couldn't get in. My SAT score was good but not great.

I got into Boston University and I wanted to go there, but we couldn't afford it. I ended up going to Indiana University, the Harvard of central Indiana. And I think I needed a phone call from my dad just to get in. I'm sure that was a proud moment for him. Even after he spent all this money on this little private school, his dumb son couldn't get into Indiana on his own.

My dad's net worth finally passed $1 million when I was in high school. In his mind, that made him a millionaire. I guess that's technically true. But when you're counting everything you own, including your car, it's not like you are sitting on a million dollars that you can go spend. It wasn't like "OK, we're millionaires. Let's go buy a pony for the kids."

What I did get, though, was an Eddie Bauer Ford Bronco II when I turned sixteen. It was maroon, with a tan stripe on the bottom. It was a great car. And it was above and beyond what my dad was used to giving a child, at least any of his first six, when they turned sixteen. He didn't have that money then. He certainly didn't buy them six new cars.

But my half sister Betsy married the son of local Ford dealer Bo Beuckman. I'm sure Bo gave us a break on it. And so here I was, driving around in this new car. I should have been grateful, and I was.

For a while.

The next year, when I was still in high school, my friend John Gregory and I tricked my mom into taking us to Lou Fusz Mazda. Next thing you know, we were talking to a dealer about a little swap. My mom couldn't say no. She loved spoiling us. We traded in my nice, solid Bronco II for a Mazda RX-7 sports car. It was an awesome car, with those pop-up headlights that made you think it was wide-eyed at you.

I'm sure my mom had to pay more for the upgrade, though I didn't realize it at the time. I just remember my dad coming home from a road trip and seeing this sports car sitting there. My Eddie Bauer Bronco II was gone, and in its place was this James Bond vehicle. That was the only time I saw my father really, really mad at me. He had worked all those jobs for all those years and bought me a nice car, and I conned my mom into trading it in for a cooler one.

I asked him, "Do you want to take a ride?"

He said, "I don't want to get in that fucking car."

"C'mon."

He got in. "All right, let me see you gun it."

I pushed the pedal down.

He was like, "That's enough. That's enough! This is the worst fucking caper of all time. This is a bunch of bullshit."

He was so mad at my mom for letting that happen. And he would just get madder.

At one point, I was driving home in that car from baseball practice, coming around a curve, and I thought, "Better slow down here. Be careful!" No, of course that's *not* what I thought. I was a teenager driving a sports car! I thought: "I just want to see what this does around a curve."

I hit the gas. It was a little bit damp. I spun out and I crashed into a little rock wall. It popped my light up. The front of the car was damaged.

I got home. My dad was so mad. He was like, "You got to be fucking kidding me. This car!"

About a week later, I parked in our driveway, behind my father's car. He got into his car to go down to the ballpark, and in his haste, he didn't realize I was parked behind him. He backed into it.

He walked inside. I was in my room, probably sleeping because I was tired from playing American Legion baseball every night. (When I would complain that I was tired, my dad would say, "Tired?!? I didn't yawn 'til I was twenty-three!") He was so furious. Now *both* cars were damaged—his and mine. It was father-on-son crime, but he would have to pay for both.

Still, I kept driving it for a little while. I took it to a party, parked behind my friend Harriet Cella's Chevy Suburban, and *she* didn't see it either. It must have been made out of the same material as a Stealth bomber. Harriet backed over the front of my car. It compressed like an accordion. One light was pointing up, one was pointing down. The car looked like a boxer who can't open one of his eyes.

Harriet walked in and said, "My dad is going to kill me. Here is a blank check. If it's more than a thousand dollars, you've got to tell me. I'll have somebody put more money in my account. But don't tell your dad, because your dad will tell my dad."

Well, I *had* to tell my dad, because my car was wrecked. It had been in three accidents in just a few weeks. It was like a big karmic "I told you so" from my father.

But also, the first two accidents suddenly didn't matter. I had a blank check from Harriet Cella to cover all the repairs. My dad got a laugh out of that.

When I was a junior in high school, I was asked to go to the prom at Mary Institute, which was the sister school to my all-boys Country Day School. My date and I did not know each other very well. I was in a high school musical production with her. I was a dorky kid, the kind of boy that girls ask to the prom when they really want to be with somebody else.

I mean, while other guys were dating girls, going to parties every weekend, I was hanging out in my friend Kevin Omell's basement and we were watching *Vacation* for the twentieth time or *Fletch* for the thirty-fifth time. Sometimes we would switch it up and play "One on One," a computer basketball game where one of us was Larry Bird and the other one was Dr. J.

We walked into the prom. My date went her way. I went mine. I ended up in this hotel room (with my friends, not my date). I think the room belonged to the girl who took my best friend, Preston Clarke, to the prom. She had connecting rooms with all the girls in her class.

I'd been to a few parties. I would drink a little bit, but never enough to get into trouble. Whenever I came home, my mom was always waiting up for me—I can still see the silhouette of her, through the window, smoking a cigarette in the kitchen. I'd have to go through this inquisition from my mom when I got home. I think that was her way of testing my lucidity. I always passed.

I was in this hotel room, and there was a big commotion in the connecting room.

Gee, what could this excitement be? Are they playing Dr. J vs. Larry Bird?

I went into the connecting room. A guy had pulled the mirror off the wall and was taking out a big bag of cocaine. He spelled *Coke is it* on the ripped-down mirror.

I spent my weekend nights pretending I was Dr. J or Larry Bird. This guy pretended he was Scarface.

A bunch of kids—mostly juniors and seniors in high school, but also some sophomores, who were invited as dates—were snorting up cocaine. Some of them were also taking Ecstasy, which was just hitting the market. I don't think it was called Ecstasy at that time. I don't know what they called it. But all these girls had popped Ecstasy and were walking around just freaking out. They were shivering, grinding their teeth—they were just so out of it.

That was not on the Country Day curriculum, and there was no test afterward. But it was probably the most important night of my high school education. I watched all these people take on different personalities and just be completely out of control because they were on drugs. I realized that I never wanted to be that out of my skull. That is why I have never used recreational drugs.[17]

---

17. Except once. I will explain later.

Chapter 4

My First Professional At-Bat

I never considered any career other than broadcasting. It just never occurred to me to do something else. If you grew up in that world, why would you ever want to leave?

From watching my dad so much, I learned the job without even realizing I was studying. But I was learning, and practicing. My dad must have liked what he heard, because on my eighteenth birthday, he decided to put me on the air alone for a half inning of radio play-by-play. It is a sign of how beloved he was in St. Louis that he could get away with it.

It was April 25, 1987. I was supposed to go to the prom at Mary Institute again. But in keeping with my prom record, the girl changed her mind. She didn't want to go with me. So my dad took me to New York instead.

I was in the back of the booth, probably thinking about the prom. I wasn't really paying attention to the game. Then I heard my father say, "Well, now, to take us through the fifth inning is my son, the birthday boy, Joe Buck."

I said, "Please don't." I'd just been dumped. That was enough humiliation for one week.

My dad and his partner, Mike Shannon, left the booth.

The inning was starting. *Somebody* had to broadcast the game.

That somebody would be me.

Thankfully, nothing interesting happened. It was a 1-2-3 inning, and lasted just a few minutes. I went back and I sat down next to the radio engineer, Colin Jarrett, and asked what he thought.

Colin said in his thick Trinidadian accent, "It lacked description."

It lacked description? It was a radio broadcast! That's like saying a painting lacks paint. Not good.

Still, on some level, I knew I could do it. I'm not saying how well—that's for others to judge. But I'd been around it so long. I'd spent a large chunk of my life in the broadcast booth. I'd be running around with Mike's son, Danny, and his daughter, Erin, who is three years younger than I am. Erin was always the cute little girl in the back of the booth.

But I had paid attention. I knew how the job was done, even though he didn't really teach me. What I mean is: He never, ever said, "OK, let's sit down tomorrow and I'm going to tell you how to broadcast." I just sat in his booth with that little earphone and I listened to him while I watched the game.

Sometimes I would go to the next booth over and do my own play-by-play into a recorder. I had access to all the game notes—the packet that teams hand to all writers and broadcasters, which include interesting tidbits and comprehensive stats. I obviously had firsthand knowledge of what the Cardinals players were doing because I was around them before the game. My dad and I would listen to that tape on the way home, and he would give me small tips about diction and grammar, and he would show me how to make one ground ball to shortstop sound different from the next grounder to shortstop. That was as close as we came to broadcasting lessons.

I was fascinated by what he did because he loved it. I think if your parent does something that he or she loves, as a kid you're automatically drawn to it because you see how happy it makes them.

I was like a kid whose parents own a diner—I knew how the lasagna was made and what to do when the place got crowded. I'm sure I did a lousy half inning of play-by-play at Shea Stadium that day, but at least I did it. I didn't panic, and my father made me do it only because he knew I could handle it.

I did not waste much time getting into the business after that. When I was still in college in 1989, I started working as the number two radio play-by-play broadcaster for the Louisville Redbirds, the Cardinals' Triple-A team. I was nineteen at the start of that season.

They didn't really need a second play-by-play guy. I don't think there was a job opening. I think they thought there was some novelty in having Jack Buck's kid broadcast their games.

I was working with an announcer named Jim Kelch. It could have been a really uncomfortable situation—Jim had ample reason to resent me. But he could not have been nicer. He grew up in Peoria, Illinois, listening to my dad, and he really welcomed me. He and his wife, Diane, had two small kids, Dan and Laura, and they basically welcomed me in as part of their family. We were all new to Louisville, as he had been broadcasting in Chattanooga for the Reds' Double-A team when he got hired.

I was making a hundred dollars a week. They just basically paid my road expenses. My father said that is when I learned the definition of the word *subsidized*, because he was helping me pay for my apartment in Louisville as I started my career.

It is also when I learned I *really* wanted to do this for a living. I loved it. The money didn't matter. I wasn't worried about who was listening to minor-league baseball. I rode a lot of buses and stayed in a lot of cheap motels. It was like *Bull Durham* except that Susan Sarandon didn't read poetry to me.

And I couldn't just show up and talk into a microphone while the support staff did everything else. We would get to the stadium, find telephone lines, put our mixer up, and put the microphones in— things that an engineer would do for my dad at Cardinals games. Then we did our own interviews and tried to get the rosters straight for the other team; unlike with the major leagues, we had no idea who most of the players were.

If we went off the air because we lost a telephone line, Jim and I had to figure out how to get back on the air. It was very primitive. It was on us to figure out how to do it. The whole experience was actually a lot harder than doing a major-league game, but I loved it.

My dad let me find my own way. I think he decided that, since he figured out how to do the job himself, I should, too. This probably made me a better broadcaster, but it also made our relationship stronger. If he hovered over me, telling me what to do, I would have hated it.

He would criticize me for only one thing: getting on the umpires. If I said, "That's a terrible call—that's not a strike," he'd look at me like, "Shut up." He taught me that umpires are professionals just like major leaguers. They work as hard at their craft. They deserve the same respect.

And you know who else deserves that respect? *Minor* leaguers. When my dad dropped me off in Louisville to broadcast Triple-A, he said, "You know, you spent your entire life watching Major League Baseball. Now you're going to the minor leagues. These guys are kids. Remember how hard the game is. Unless you believe you could have made that play ten times out of ten, don't act like you could do it."

It was such great advice. Some announcers rip players—Harry Caray did it a lot. He would openly say, "How in the heck can you miss that fly ball?" I've tried to avoid that.

But it was the only big advice my dad gave me. My mom is the real critic. I call her when I want an honest assessment. My father always said something like "That's great," and left it at that. Even when I was an adult, he was my buddy more than my father. Buddies don't critique each other.

That season, I got a chance to fill in as color commentator on a Cardinals game. That meant I was supposed to analyze what happened in a major-league game for a TV audience. That was new for me. A color commentator doesn't have to be as polished a broadcaster as the play-by-play guy, but he needs to have more knowledge of the game. A play-by-play announcer may tell you the runner is taking a big lead off of first base, but the color commentator has to tell you why stealing a base makes sense in that situation.

I knew this was going to be really different. When you go on TV, you put on a fancy suit, make sure your hair is just right,[18] cake some makeup on your face while somebody sets up the lighting to make you look good, put in an earpiece, listen to a producer count down until you can go on the air, and then introduce a prerecorded video piece.

When you go on the radio, you . . . go on the radio. That's it. Sit at the microphone and speak. You don't even have to wear pants, though I usually do.

Television is an act. Radio is about being yourself. On the radio, you just start painting a picture, for lack of a less pretentious term. In TV the picture is already painted, and you just add the happy little trees.[19] Television announcing is, by its very nature, redundant: As long as viewers can see the screen, they don't really need the play-by-play announcer.

On the radio, there is no ground ball to second base until the radio announcer says, "Ground ball to second base." It can be a smash or a one-hopper or a flare or a slow roller, but that's for the announcer to decide. On TV, if you see a ground ball to second base, and I say, "Ground ball to second base," the appropriate reaction, as a viewer, is "No shit. I just saw that." That's why I tell anybody getting into the TV business: The camera really does the play-by-play. You just accentuate it.

A lot of times, I won't say the score at the end of an inning, espe-

---

18. OK, I fix my hair for the radio, too.
19. Shout out to my man, the late Bob Ross, and his show, *The Joy of Painting*.

cially if it's a big moment in an important game. I let the video tell the story. I've gotten letters from visually impaired people ripping me for not giving enough information.

So radio allows for more creativity, but in a way, TV is more complicated. You can get away with more on radio. You can miss something by a second and nobody will know. On TV, you had better be on it. In radio, the announcers run the show. In TV, there are producers and a lot more moving parts.

But back then, I didn't know all of this—I was just excited for the opportunity and the differences, too. I was paired with Ken Wilson, who held the distinction of being one of the few people in the world who hated my dad. I think he was jealous. At one point, somebody compared Wilson to my dad, and Wilson responded by doing a mocking imitation of him for an entire inning of a Cardinals game. It's kind of amazing that he got away with that.

As you can imagine, a man who did not like Jack Buck *really* didn't like working with Jack's college-punk son. To be fair, I had no business doing color commentary on a major-league game. I had never done it on any level, I was in college, and color commentators are usually former major-league players. It was silly to ask me to analyze everything happening on the field. I was just as qualified to write international trade agreements.

But here we were. He had no choice.

We were in Montreal. Before the game, I was walking behind Wilson by the batting cage, and he said to Mike Shannon, "Well, Mike, it looks like it's my turn to babysit tonight."

That stung. I don't even remember the game—just Wilson's comment.

———————

I think my dad was proud that I was willing to go to Triple-A at age nineteen and make $400 a month. That salary included my duties as the club's traveling secretary. I was giving per diem money to players—some pretty well-known, like Leon Durham and Terry Francona, some prospects like Bernard Gilkey and Ray Lankford, and some career minor leaguers. There was no glamour in it. I think my father could see that I wasn't doing this just because I grew up around it. I really enjoyed it as much as he did.

Todd Zeile, the Cardinals' prized catching prospect, was on that Louisville team, and we hit it off. Late in that 1989 season, he was called up to the major-league club, and the next season, I got my own taste of major-league life.

The first game I ever did play-by-play for the Cardinals was in New York in 1990. That was when I slapped too much makeup on my face and sweated so much that my earpiece fell out.

The next year, I left Indiana University. My dad paid for all those years of Country Day, and now his kid was a college dropout. He couldn't complain too much, though. I had a good reason: I was going to call Cardinals games on the radio with him and Mike Shannon.

As I got ready to go back to St. Louis, my personal life took a radical turn. My high school girlfriend, Ann Archambault, called me. Her mom had cancer. She was dying.

Ann[20] and I had remained good friends after high school. I felt a

———————

20. Ann was not one of the girls who ditched me for prom. She went to St. Joseph's Academy, and we dated off and on in high school but never went to my prom together.

strong urge to take care of her, because I cared so much about her and this was such a terrible time in her life. We started dating again—long-distance, because she was in college. In 1991, I rented an apartment so that I wasn't living with my parents while I was broadcasting for the Cardinals. Soon after, I bought a house, thinking: "This is where Ann and I will live." I just kind of assumed that she and I were going to get engaged. And we did.

We were twenty-three years old when we got married. It was a big wedding. My dad was the master of ceremonies, in essence. Stan Musial was there, playing his harmonica. Dan Dierdorf was there. We hired a band, but they barely had to play because one entertainer after another told stories. One of Ann's classmates was dating a minor-league catcher named Mike Matheny, who now manages the Cardinals. Sometimes, St. Louis can seem like a one-stoplight town.

I confided in Ann. I told her about my fears of broadcasting failure. She supported me, and off we went, on a journey that we expected to last forever.

Meanwhile, my professional life was taking off. Stepping into the broadcast booth with my dad and Mike was bizarre. I had spent so much time with both of them through the years that I considered them Dad and Other Dad.

But there were definitely some adjustments to make. One problem was that I didn't even know what to call them. I couldn't call my dad "Dad" on the air—that would be like reminding the world that I was his kid. And I had never called Mike Shannon "Mike." It was "Mr. Shannon." That wasn't going to work on the air either. I finally settled on "Mike" for Shannon. I never really addressed my father as anything. It was "Hey, you . . ." or "Great point, and" . . . like he was nameless. I hoped nobody would notice.

My dad and Mike were a broadcast team, but they were also great friends. And like a lot of great friends, they went through stretches where they wanted to kill each other. I believe it was Walt Whitman, or perhaps Grantland Rice, who wrote, "A baseball season is really fucking long."

It can seem longer when your partner is Mike Shannon. Understand: I love the man. I actually learned more baseball from Mike than I learned from my dad. He taught me about game situations, when to hold against runners, how to pitch certain guys, how to position outfielders—the overall feel of what a team is trying to do.

But Mike is an in-your-face presence. He always has deals going—he's setting up golf, he's setting up fishing, he wants to go out to dinner. He craves action. My father was different. He enjoyed the rare moments when he didn't have to play "Jack Buck"—he liked to sit on the bus or in hotel lobbies and read biographies.

Even though my dad was a people person, and he would talk to strangers anytime and anywhere, he was not really the center of the social whirl with the Cardinals. That was the players' place. He would sleep on a plane with his mouth open and a Stim-U-Dent toothpick dangling out of it. Then he'd wake up and play cards with Herzog, the Cardinals manager. Or he would read his book.

But when we were out in the city, *any* city, he would talk to people. I don't know if it felt like part of his duty as the broadcaster for the

Cardinals, or he just thoroughly enjoyed interacting with random people. Probably both.

My dad was the broadcasting pro—naturally eloquent, capable of doing any event. Mike was . . . different. Mike grew up in St. Louis, briefly played quarterback for Missouri, and played for the Cardinals before retiring at age thirty because of nephritis. When I was little, he would come to our house to get broadcasting tips from my dad because his grammar was so poor. But he became this larger-than-life local radio guy who people enjoy listening to because it's comforting.

When you do the home team's games, you don't have to be as refined as Vin Scully or Ernie Harwell. You can be quirky and endearing. If you grow up in St. Louis, you know that when you hear Mike Shannon, it's time to chill and enjoy a ball game.

And you never know what you're going to hear. One time, we were doing a Cardinals-Astros game, and Mike said, "Thomas Howard hasn't stolen a base since . . ."

Since what?

Since May 3?

Since he injured his toe?

". . . the Jupiter invasion."

Then he ended it with "Right?"

I was like, "Uh, yeah, Mike. Right. He hasn't stolen a base since the Jupiter invasion. You took the words right out of my mouth."

A lot of Cardinals fans thought Mike was drunk during games. He wasn't. I never saw him work while drunk. I never even saw him have one drink in the booth. He would just say wacky shit sometimes. I loved it, and I think fans did, too. It doesn't hurt anybody to have a little diversion in a three-hour broadcast. I would listen to other broadcast teams, and I would think, "God, that's just so straightforward—so blah, so bland." Our booth was never bland. Baseball is not math class. It's supposed to be fun.

Another time, I read a note on the air, welcoming a few hundred French foreign exchange students to the ballpark.

Mike said, "I wonder where they're from."

I said, "France?"

He said, "Yeah. You know, they say if you can speak French, you can speak any of those languages over there. It's not like Chinese, because they got a million different derelicts."

I said, "You mean dialects."

He said, "Yeah, I mean dialects. But they got a million derelicts, too."

Meanwhile, I was trying to tell people what was happening in a baseball game, pitch by pitch.

You can have a lot of wild times on the road with a major-league team when you are young, but since I was in a serious relationship that quickly led to marriage, I wasn't all that wild. I was enjoying life on the road with a major-league team in my own dorky way. Zeile was still my good friend, and we were traveling around together in the major leagues. So we struck a deal.

At the time, most players had to room together. The collective bargaining agreement did not mandate that each player got his own room. If they wanted their own room, they had to pay the difference.

I was a member of the media as the Cardinals announcer, so I got my own room. (Imagine that: the media getting better perks than the players.)

Zeile said, "Hey, you and I are hanging out anyway. I need a roommate." He wasn't close to many teammates, so he wasn't dying to room with any of them. And he didn't want to pay to get a single room, partly because he wasn't interested in picking up groupies and bringing them back. He was married to Julianne McNamara, the Olympic gymnast, whom he met at UCLA.

And so Todd and I ended up rooming together. I didn't think much of it. I was happy to be in the big leagues, and Todd was a good friend. I was glad to help him out.

Not everybody saw it that way. Joe Torre was the Cardinals manager, and one day when we were on the road, Joe called Todd and me into his office.

He said, "Look, I really don't care that you guys are in the same room. I get it. Todd, you don't want to pay for a single room. But some of the guys on the team don't like a player being such close friends with an announcer on the team."

It didn't even dawn on me that this was weird until Joe said so. But as soon as he said it, I understood. Why would they be comfortable with it? We were crossing a line we shouldn't have crossed. Zeile wasn't passing state secrets to me, but it was a bad look.

Two or three years later, there were rumors that Todd and I roomed together because we were gay. It was a long time ago, but I'm pretty confident we never slept together. This seems like the kind of thing I would remember.

You would think that, in 1991, if an announcer and a player *were* gay lovers, they would be smart enough not to share a room on the road. I mean, that wouldn't be very discreet.

Anyway, the rumor was false, but it was out there. There was nothing I could do about it. And it wouldn't be the last time I dealt with a rumor like that.

When the Cardinals hired me, I was supposed to just do the weekend games on the radio. But that quickly changed. Tom Barton, the former radio engineer who had been promoted to run the broadcast, told me to do a few innings of *every* game on the radio, and keep doing it unless somebody above him complained about it. So I would do some play-by-play while my dad did color for me, or Mike Shannon would do play-by-play while I did color. We rotated inning by inning.

The job itself did not intimidate me. I had taken those steps into the KMOX booth since I was able to walk. There was no mystery to it. I literally moved one seat over, exchanged the single canned headphones for a microphone, and joined the broadcast. To others, it looked like I was overpromoted. For me, it felt totally natural.

Meanwhile, my dad's career had taken its own exciting turn. He was supposed to be on CBS's number two major-league broadcasting team with Jim Kaat, which would have been great for him. He and Kaat loved each other. They would have been a good listen, too. It would have been a good team.

But then, right before the 1990 season started, CBS fired Brent Musburger. He was supposed to be the number one play-by-play guy for baseball, along with their number one guy for pretty much everything else. That stunned the industry, and it left a hole in CBS's major-league lineup. They moved my dad up. He would get to call the top games, including the playoffs and the World Series, for a national TV audience.

I felt like we were both getting the chance of a lifetime. But it turned out not to be so pleasant for either of us.

Chapter 5

Cold Winds

Early in my time with the Cardinals, I was stunned to pick up my hometown paper, the *St. Louis Post-Dispatch*, and see this headline:

BUCKING DUES: ANNOUNCER'S SON MUST EARN CARDS SPOT

Dan Caesar, the media critic at the *Post-Dispatch*, wrote:

The burning question is why is Joe Buck, at age 21, being force-fed to Cardinals fans? Why is a kid, still in college, showing up on what many broadcast people consider the premier local team network in baseball? The reason is simple. And it's spelled B-U-C-K . . . What's most offensive about the situation is Joe Buck's lack of dues-paying.

It was hard to read that in the only paper in my town, as a twenty-one-year-old. I felt like I got torpedoed before I even got started. I was so devastated that I actually cried.

A few weeks into the season, Caesar criticized me again. Then he asked for an interview.

I said, "Dan, you have my permission to just make up my quotes. I've got nothing to say. So if you want to make it up, I'm giving you free rein."

He said, "Well, what does that mean?"

"It means I'm not interested in talking to you. You're going to write whatever you want. You haven't even really given me a chance. So just make it up. Go ahead."

He asked if he could take me to lunch to try to talk it out. We met at some restaurant at the mall. I told him: "I realize I'm being sensitive. I realize I'm my dad's kid. But give me a chance. Let me do it and then tell St. Louis if I'm good or not good."

And you know what? He did. He gave me a chance. And we got along great after that. But I kept that first article in my wallet for many years.

Meanwhile, my dad was having his own difficulties. He never seemed comfortable in the CBS booth, and he didn't do his best work there. One reason was that, when he got called up to the number one team, Jim Kaat did not go with him. My father had to work with the network's lead color guy: Tim McCarver.

I don't know when the problems between Tim and my dad started.

But they were obvious to me as I watched the games. One time, as CBS showed a shot of flags flying in the outfield, my dad said on the air, "As you can see, the wind is blowing out to left."

Tim said, "Jack, I have to correct you on that. You can't *see* the wind. You can see the *effect* of the wind."

I remember thinking: "But you can *see* that Tim McCarver is being a dick."

Tim nitpicked everything my dad did. It seemed clear he didn't want him there. One time, when I was doing minor-league games in Louisville, Jim Kelch and I drove to visit my dad in the booth in Cincinnati for an afternoon game.

I walked into the booth.

My father said, "Say hi to Tim."

I did, but it was a cold, almost angry hello.

And even though my dad was a Baseball Hall of Famer, Tim was considered the star at CBS. He was the country's premier baseball announcer at the time, and in many ways he would set the standard for color announcers for the next twenty years. Tim was the fair-haired boy. He would even help anchor the Olympics broadcast in 1992.

My dad? He was the aging radio-turned-TV-play-by-play guy, and he couldn't be himself. His voice sounded different. It sounded squeezed to me. It didn't have the same life. He didn't have the same laugh. His sense of humor didn't translate. In their booth, he was supposed to be the setup man, not the closer.

He grew up listening to radio, not watching TV. He came up in the business in the 1960s—a wilder time, carefree in ways that are hard to imagine today. When he did the Ice Bowl in Green Bay in 1967, he needed something to warm him up. He drank coffee, and the stuff he poured in it was *not* half-and-half. Drinking alcohol on the job was not scandalous—it was almost expected at that time. Certainly it was accepted. He and a couple of other broadcasters flew out of Green Bay on a rented plane. Just after takeoff, the door opened, and they landed in a cornfield—and they *laughed* about it. It was just a wilder time in so many ways.

Now he was in this staid broadcast, and he didn't fit. It just was weird. I was watching, thinking, "That's not him." It's strange to watch your father on national TV, not acting like himself. And it's not fun.

People noticed he was struggling, and if they didn't, Rudy Martzke was there to remind them.

The name Rudy Martzke doesn't mean much to sports fans today. I don't even know how much it meant to sports fans in 1990. But if you were in the media—or if your dad was—that name could send chills down your spine and make you so nauseated you wanted to skip breakfast.

Rudy was the sports TV critic for *USA Today*. These days, there are a million sports TV critics, from the actual professionals to bloggers to the fan who makes one snarky comment on Twitter that gets retweeted three thousand times.

Back then, there weren't many TV sports critics, and Martzke was by far the most powerful. I maintain, to this day, that the average person didn't read his column. But everybody in the sports television industry went right to it every Monday. It was a recap of the weekend. He seemed like someone who could make or break your career in about three words. It was a big deal to be in that column. I think I had been the only kid at Indiana who subscribed to *USA Today*. I wanted to see what Martzke said about my father.

Rudy and my dad had some history together. It was not good history. My dad got sideways on a financial deal with somebody who was a friend of Rudy's.

This was in the early seventies in St. Louis. My dad borrowed money for our first house from somebody who was . . . what's the best way to describe this? *Of questionable reputation.* My dad paid the guy back, but then he was kind of intertwined with this guy. He was not the kind of gentleman with whom you would want to be intertwined. Law-enforcement officers came to my father to ask about this person.

Then somebody else came to my father and he said, "You have a nice young new wife, huh?"

My dad said, "Uh-huh."

The guy said, "You have a little boy. What's his name? Joe?"

"Yep."

He said, "Yeah, we're keeping an eye on that."

So there was basically a threat of a mob hit put out on me when I was a kid. My dad told the cigar-smoking chief of detectives of St. Louis, a friend of his named John Doherty. Colonel Doherty went to this gentleman and said, "If Jack's son, Joe, skins his knee, you're dead."

I know what you're thinking: "That wasn't your childhood, Joe. That was an episode of *Columbo*." But I swear, this actually happened.

Well, Rudy Martzke had St. Louis ties—in the seventies, he became the director of operations for the Spirits of St. Louis, the American Basketball Association team. He was friends with the guy who loaned my dad the money. So when my father became the lead baseball voice for CBS, and Rudy was the nation's premier sports TV critic, there was already some bad blood there.

The biggest criticism of my dad was that he anticipated plays too much, and sometimes they didn't unfold the way he expected: "That ball is out of here . . . no! He caught it!" He could get away with that on the radio in St. Louis, but when he did it on national TV, people crushed him for it.

Once, he thought a runner would be safe at home and he said, "They're not gonna get him!" But they did get him.

McCarver was not impressed, and he was undermining him. In the eyes of most people at the time, McCarver could do no wrong. Every mistake my father made got magnified, and since he was so uncomfortable, he made more mistakes than he ever had. And his age was starting to show for the first time—not so much because he lost his fastball but because his sensibilities were 1970s and local, and he was broadcasting in the 1990s for a national audience.

Before one game of the 1990 National League Championship Series in Pittsburgh, singer Bobby Vinton sang the national anthem. Well, he sang most of it. He flubbed some of the lyrics, and the melody, but the crowd cheered for him anyway, and my dad, on CBS, cracked, "Well, when you're Polish and live in Pittsburgh, you can do anything you want with the words."

I was in college, watching with my buddy Lee Dabagia. Lee said, "He's going to get some shit for that." And he did. He got back to his hotel room that night and there was a footprint smashed into his pillow. He was really just trying to make a joke to take the heat off of Bobby Vinton, who screwed up the anthem. It might have worked on local radio in 1975, but it was the wrong joke to make on national TV in 1990. He got ripped for that. The pressure on him was rising. It was hard for our family to take.

At the end of the 1991 Cardinals season, as my dad got ready to do the playoffs for CBS, I rode out to California with Todd Zeile in his Jeep. It was a costly trip for me. I had injured my back playing pickup basketball and my L5-S1 disc, the very bottom disc, was bulging. It was cutting off the nerve to my left leg. By the time we got out there, I was in so much pain.

I went to a KC and The Sunshine Band concert with a guy named Bo Howell and a college friend of my buddy Preston. Preston went to Kansas. His friend's name was Paul Rudd.

I always enjoyed hanging out with Paul, just as I always enjoyed hanging out with a friend Preston had introduced me to in high school. His name was Jon Hamm.

Today, the names Paul Rudd and Jon Hamm are familiar to most of you. At the time, they were just guys I knew. Preston's sister, Sarah, actually dated both of them, though not at the same time. Sarah ended up being a successful actress herself, but you gotta admit, when it came to her dating life, she was a hell of a casting director.

But back then, dating Jon Hamm and Paul Rudd was not that big a deal. We were just all in the same circle. When Preston would visit me at Indiana, he would bring his buddy Paul with him. Rudd had long, flowing hair—like, down to the middle of his back. We hung out and hit it off. We became instant friends.

Anyway, the day after the concert, I couldn't sit up. That nerve to my leg had shut off. If I tried to sit up, my leg would just flop. I had paramedics take me out of the house, and I spent two days in a Hollywood hospital, and that's where I watched Game 6 of the World Series between the Twins and the Braves.

That's the game that ended with Twins star Kirby Puckett hitting a game-winning home run to force Game 7 the next day. As it cleared the fence in the Metrodome, my dad made one of the most famous calls of his career:

"And we will see you tomorrow night!"

The call was just perfect. It was memorable, spontaneous, unique, and got right to the point of what that home run meant. He didn't even have to tell viewers to tune in for Game 7, because it was implied.

As I watched in my hospital room, I was in awe. That's a hard home run to call, and here is why: Puckett's ball had to clear a Plexiglas wall at the Metrodome. But behind the Plexiglas were people in white shirts waving these white Homer Hankies that the Twins gave out that year. From the broadcast booth, it's virtually impossible to tell where the top of a Plexiglas wall is. It's hard to tell the difference between a ball hitting the wall and coming back, or going over. And if you wait to make sure it's gone, you can lose the timing that makes it a great call.

My dad didn't wait. As soon as the ball cleared the Plexiglas: "And we will see you tomorrow night!"

As I watched on TV, I thought, "Man, that was a hell of a call."

It reminded me of his call when Ozzie Smith hit a game-winning home run against Tom Niedenfuer in the 1985 National League

Championship Series. Ozzie, a switch-hitter, was batting lefty. Ozzie had never hit a left-handed home run in his career. He hit this one down the line, off a cement pillar above the wall. It bounced back on the field, and the Dodgers right fielder fielded it and threw it in, like he was trying to fool the umpire. A lot of announcers would have been fooled, too, or at least would have paused.

Yet my father saw it right away, and he told fans on the Cardinals broadcast: "Go crazy, folks! Go crazy!" If you walk up to a Cardinals fan today, three decades later, and say, "Go crazy, folks!" that fan will know exactly what you mean.

Viewers don't think about this, but broadcasters do: You can't be wrong in a big moment like Kirby Puckett's home run. That stains you for a lifetime in this business. If my dad had said, "We will see you tomorrow night!" and the ball actually bounced off the wall for a double instead of a game-ending home run, he would have been fired. I'm sure of it.

And the reason I'm sure is that he was fired anyway.

He did Game 7 with McCarver, an all-time classic—Jack Morris pitched ten shutout innings for the Twins, who beat John Smoltz and the Braves 1–0. That was the last baseball game my dad did for CBS. We all knew it was over. I felt terrible for him, but I felt a little relieved, too.

After my dad was fired, I wrote him this long letter that he kept with him. I wrote, "*I know this is eating you up.*" Every Monday, Martzke would nitpick his mistakes and drop his age in the column to let viewers know he thought my old man was washed up: "Jack Buck, 65 . . ." or "Jack Buck, 66 . . ."

He had gone from local to national and from radio to TV, and that was hard to do. It all drove him into being somebody that he wasn't. He worried about what he was saying. He knew if he said something wrong, or even if he didn't, Tim might give him a verbal smackdown on the air. It's a tough way to do that job.

In my letter, I told him that he had already hit the broadcasting equivalent of a game-ending home run with his call on Puckett's homer. He had accomplished so much in his career. It was time for him to put a towel around his neck and enjoy himself—sit on the dugout bench and just take it all in.

Of course, he didn't do that. This was a man who would interrupt his own dinner to chat with fans. He never really shut it off. He wasn't about to change just because he got fired. He kept doing Cardinals games, and I was so lucky that I got to do them with him for parts of eleven seasons. I got a lot of that time back that I'd lost when he was away.

I was on the charter with him. I was on the team bus with him. I was in the team hotel with him. Wherever the Cardinals played, I was in the booth with him and Mike Shannon.

And we had so much fun. Once, at a breakfast program for people who ran the Cardinals' TV and radio affiliates, I teased him about his ugly sport coat.[21] I should have known better than to start a one-liner war with my father. He stepped to the mic and said that after he

---

21. My dad was color-blind, which led to some poor fashion decisions.

found out I was a bed wetter, he bought me an electric blanket for Christmas.

I got to see firsthand the people he touched and the way he treated people in this business. Some broadcasters would blow right by people, but he made a connection with everyone in his path.

This is a competitive business. There are only so many jobs, and there are many more people who want them. It can lead to some ugly moments. But I've never had to worry when somebody said, "Oh, I worked with your dad once." I knew the next line was never, ever going to be "He treated me like crap." It was usually "I've never worked with a nicer guy in my life."

Part 3

Thanks, Mr. Murdoch

Chapter 6

A Fourth Network

In December 1993, after my third year of doing Cardinals games, I got a huge break. But I didn't realize it at first. I was too baffled to understand what was happening.

I was hosting a call-in show for KMOX when the news came across the wire: FOX had won the rights to the NFL's NFC package. I couldn't believe it. *FOX?* FOX didn't do major events. That's because FOX wasn't a major network. It was where you found Joan Rivers, an adult cartoon show called *The Simpsons*, and Al Bundy sticking his hand down his pants on *Married . . . with Children*.

The NFL belonged on CBS, where Pat Summerall reminded viewers to "stay tuned for *60 Minutes*—except on the West Coast." And other than *Monday Night Football*, the NFC was the jewel of the NFL's

TV packages—the conference had won ten straight Super Bowls and featured most of the league's marquee teams and biggest markets.

I expressed my astonishment and outrage to the tens of people who were listening to my show that night. KMOX was owned and operated by CBS. My listeners and I deserved an explanation!

The explanation came soon enough: "Hey, dumbass! Rupert Murdoch wrote a bigger check."

Oh, is *that* how it works?

I was so busy being upset that I didn't think about the fact that FOX would need *announcers* for these games. And I was an *announcer*. And . . .

Hey, wait a minute!

What if . . .

FOX Sports was run by an Australian named David Hill. He was basically building a network sports division from scratch. That was a big task, but it also meant David had the freedom and budget to hire the best people in the business. And since CBS no longer had an NFL package, David could poach a lot of CBS's best talent.

David quickly hired the great Ed Goren of CBS to be his top lieutenant. Then David and Ed hired CBS's top NFL broadcast team of Summerall and John Madden. That was brilliant, not just because they were the best, but because everybody *knew* they were the best. That shut up a lot of critics. It brought FOX Sports instant credibility. Fans could stop worrying that Bart Simpson would broadcast the Super Bowl. It was like if people said you couldn't put together a rock band, and then you brought in Mick Jagger and Keith Richards.

David also hired producer Bob Stenner and director Sandy Grossman, who worked with Summerall and Madden at CBS. That was also brilliant. It smoothed the transition for Summerall and Madden.

FOX would have as many as seven games a week. Summerall and Madden would do the best matchup, for the biggest audience. Then David hired Dick Stockton and Matt Millen for the number two team.

That was a great start. But it was only a start. FOX Sports was like an expansion team that spends big money on top free agents but doesn't have a farm system. Hill had to hire a bunch of lower-level announcers and producers—and quick.

Was I interested? I guess so, in the sense that *everybody* was interested. I didn't think I had a chance. I didn't really think I deserved one. I'd never done the NFL. I'd also never done college football. Or high school football. Or Tecmo Bowl. I'd never done football in my life.

At the Super Bowl a few weeks later, the most popular man in town was Ed Goren. Everybody and their mothers bombarded him with audition tapes.

Well, in my case, it was just my mother.

I did not attend the Super Bowl. But my dad was there to do the game for CBS radio, and my mom went with him, and she brought a tape of my work to give to Ed's wife, Patti, whom she knew. My mom said, "You really ought to hear my son, Joe. He's good at doing baseball." All I had really done was baseball and college basketball, unless you count the time I did a horse-jumping show, and what the heck, let's just count that. It was not the best horse-jumping broadcast in history, but I studied enough to fake my way through it.

My mom never told me she was bringing a tape to Patti Goren. She didn't tell my dad, either. I think she knew he wouldn't approve. He would have told her to mind her own business.

Ed liked what he heard on the tape. But there was still the small problem that I had never done football. So he invited me to do a live audition at the new FOX football studio to see if I was any good.

To help me get ready, my dad had a videotape of a Saints game sent to us by a CBS affiliate in St. Louis. Bobby Hebert was the quarterback. My father and I sat in a living room in Florida during spring training and I did the game off TV with him. He had done decades of football over the years. I thought he was even better at football than he was at baseball. He had done *Monday Night Football* on the radio with Hall of Fame coach Hank Stram, and he did the NFL for CBS television and other networks. He was trying to teach me how to do it. He told me I was saying too much for a television presentation. I was telling our imaginary viewers the Saints were in the I-formation, or had split backs, or so-and-so was lined up in the slot. My dad said to keep it simple. I'd announce the down and distance, and maybe point out if a receiver was in motion, then be quiet until the play developed. I didn't need to say, "Hebert drops back to pass." Anybody watching the game could see he dropped back to pass.

I went out to Los Angeles to audition. I was twenty-three.

I rarely get nervous for a broadcast, but I was nervous for that audition. I knew it would determine the next chunk of my career, and maybe my life. I was young and married, with no kids and a huge opportunity in front of me.

At the audition in a television studio, I was introduced to Tim Green, who was just out of the game and was tackling his law degree. He obviously knew the game but had never broadcast anything in his life. At least I had been a broadcaster. Tim hadn't done *anything*.

At one point, they told us if we hit the talk-back button, we could talk to the producer, Bob Stenner.

Tim said, "What's the talk-back button?"

He had no idea. This would be like getting on the pitcher's mound, and the manager says to get the signal from the catcher, and you say, "Which one is the catcher?"

But I couldn't fault Tim. It was all new to him.

We would watch video of a game from the previous season and do a fake broadcast. They gave us the names, numbers, heights, weights, and colleges for all the players—all the stuff broadcasters would typically get.

Once we started rolling, I was not nervous. I was a little bit out of my element, but I figured everybody was. It's weird doing a game off TV in a studio. But the pressure didn't cripple me. They rolled the game and pumped in fake crowd noise, and we just did it. This wasn't radio. I didn't have to create this picture for listeners. I had to accent the action.

I knew, as the game went along, that it was going well. I was young, but I had been around the business long enough to know when a broadcast is going well and when it's not. I felt comfortable, not rushed or forced. I was anticipating the action and getting my facts right. I felt like I did during a baseball game—whatever happened, I knew what to say.

When Tim and I finished, we put our headsets down. George Krieger, an executive who worked with Ed and David, told me: "We're going to hire you. Do you have an agent?"

I thought: "An agent. Right. I guess I need one of those."

I hired Jim Steiner. He didn't have any broadcasting clients, but he lived in St. Louis and I knew him. He didn't have much leverage with FOX. There was no competition for my services. Jim got me a few perks, which I appreciated, but that was all he could realistically do. FOX thought I was lucky to be hired at all, and FOX was right.

Tim Green did not get an offer that day. He and I went to Denny's after our audition and we sat there: me knowing I was getting hired, him unsure. I was excited, but I couldn't let it show, because I didn't want him to feel bad. But pretty soon, he did get an offer from FOX. And we were paired together for two years, which was great.

We did one preseason game as practice. It never aired—it was just for us to get some work in. I called the game exhibition football on the (fake) air, and I was told that was wrong. It was *preseason*. Apparently, that sounds more important.

Our first real game was the 1994 season opener at Soldier Field. As I heard somebody in my earpiece counting down to the first segment, I thought: "What in the hell have I gotten myself into?" I didn't know if I could do it. But within a few minutes, I stopped thinking about it. I just did the game.

Tim was so new to broadcasting that I was basically his on-air tutor. When he said something, I would give him a thumbs-up or thumbs-down—you can only imagine how the old-guard TV critics would have reacted if they knew that. And I didn't even really know what I was doing. So my dad would tell me what to tell Tim, and then I would tell him.

But Tim listened to me. I've learned, working with a lot of ex-athletes on the air, that for the most part they want a scoreboard. They want to be critiqued. They are used to being coached, and they want that. I don't overdo it, but when it's appropriate, I will say something.

Summerall and Madden were the number one team. Dick Stockton and Matt Millen were number two. We were the number three or four team, depending on who was doing the ranking. But I felt we would only move up over time. I hit it off with the executives. I felt comfortable.

I also felt I was working at the right network. Only FOX would have hired me at that age to do the NFL when I had never done football.

I quickly learned that it was great to work for a place that was starting from scratch, because FOX was not married to some of the stupid policies that were standard at other networks. Everybody in the history of the sports broadcasting business had fudged expense reports. FOX's solution: no expense reports. We got a certain number of dollars per day. FOX had a car service pick us up at the airport and take us where we needed to go. Nobody could claim it took six cabs and $427 to get from the airport to the Hyatt. FOX cut the bullshit.

The first year was as seamless as I could have hoped. I really was just trying to get through it without anybody realizing I didn't know what I was doing. Thankfully, I was about to get some help.

Tim Green and I did a practice preseason game in Chicago in 1995. After it, I was walking out of the stadium when a long-haired man shook my hand and said:

"I wanted to introduce myself. I'm Steve Horn. I knew your grandfather. I know your dad. I've worked for [Bob] Costas forever. I work at FOX now. If you ever need anything, give me a call."

Horn was doing editorial consulting for FOX NFL Sunday. He was a behind-the-scenes guy, helping with story lines and finding material for the announcers on the pregame show. He had this huge network of scouts for NFL and baseball to tell him what was really going on. He would tell the announcer how a pitcher adjusted his grip for his breaking ball, or why a quarterback wasn't the right fit for his new offense—stuff you usually don't see in a newspaper but which is invaluable for broadcasters.

I called Horn a couple of times early in my time at FOX, to get a different angle on whatever game I was covering that I was doing with Tim Green. I did not yet realize that he would become one of the most important people in my career, and in my life.

In November 1995, FOX landed another big sports-rights deal: The network would share rights to Major League Baseball with NBC. This did not stun the industry like the NFL deal. FOX had already shown it could do sports. People had already learned they could find FOX on their TV as easily as they could find CBS or ABC if they wanted to watch a game.

And this time, I knew right away that I wanted to be part of the broadcasting mix. I was established as a football announcer with FOX already. Suddenly, I had an advantage over every other job candidate: I was in-house, and I had done a lot of baseball. I had done all

162 Cardinals games per year before I started doing football for FOX, and I was still doing 140. I knew as soon as FOX got baseball that I would be involved. This wasn't like when FOX got the NFL, and it never occurred to me that I might work there.

FOX made me the lead play-by-play announcer, which meant I would do the *Game of the Week* on Saturdays, playoff games, and the World Series when FOX had it. It was a dream, except for one detail.

My partner.

Tim McCarver.

I think it's fair to say Tim would not have been my first choice. He would not have been in my top 100, to be honest, and it had nothing to do with his ability. I knew he was very good. But I think you get more protective of your family than of yourself, and I was still upset with how Tim had treated my dad—more upset, I think, than my dad was.

This had the potential to be awkward. But what was I going to do? I certainly wasn't going to turn down the chance to broadcast the World Series on national TV because of an old grudge.

I decided Tim and I needed to clear the air. Before the season started, we went to our first FOX baseball seminar. Then we went to dinner as part of a big group. I said, "Come over here." At the time, I was twenty-six. He was fifty-four. He was the veteran. I didn't care. I said, "Look, we need to have a drink. Let's just figure this out now."

We had a drink, and I said, "I know things didn't go well with my dad. But you and I are going to be judged on how we do together. You know what I think of my dad, how I adore him. But I'm bigger than that. You're bigger than that. Let's just go forward and see what we do together as Joe and Tim, not Jack and Tim, or not Jack's son, Joe. Just Joe and Tim."

We shook hands. He was great. We never discussed what happened between him and my father. There was no need. We both knew it hadn't worked. And he had talked to Mike Shannon, and Shannon told him, "You're going to love working with Joe. He's different than Jack." I think Tim went in with a good attitude. We hit it off immediately. I loved working with Tim. We never had one cross word in the eighteen years we worked together.

I would never have predicted this in 1991, but Tim McCarver became a friend. He is my friend, to this day. But we are not the kind of friends who socialize together. This story may help explain why.

Shortly after we were paired, we went out for dinner the night before a game in Boston. I was late to dinner.[22] So I was the last one in our party to arrive at this seafood restaurant. Everybody else was already seated.

I took the only open seat, next to our producer, John "Flip" Filippelli. Filippelli and McCarver never got along, pretty much from the moment they started working together. They clashed nonstop, to the point where I, the guy in his twenties, was basically mediator between Tim and Flip. It was awkward. I was still trying to find my way, and I had to make sure that the producer and the main analyst wouldn't punch each other.

I'd never witnessed anything like it in this profession. I tried to tap-

---

22. I am always late to dinner.

dance back and forth to ease the tension without violating anybody's trust. Later, we were in Cleveland before a playoff game, and we were supposed to meet at a production truck, and Tim got there a few minutes late, and Flip snapped at him for it. But Tim had been talking to players in the clubhouse. It wasn't like he was goofing around. Stuff like that happened all the time.

I felt like Filippelli should have tried a little harder to get along with Tim, since Tim was the one performing on air and really was the one who gave us credibility. But that was between them.

Anyway, I sat down with Flip, Tim, and the crew. I ordered this huge lobster claw, and when I finished the meat, the claw was dripping in butter. I wrapped a napkin around it, and while Filippelli was looking the other way, I slipped the lobster claw wrapped in the napkin into the inside pocket of the blazer on the back of his chair. I was giggling to myself. I wasn't that far removed from being a Sigma Nu[23] at Indiana, and even though I never graduated from college, I got a master's degree in doing stupid shit to my friends for my own amusement. Flip and I had the kind of relationship where we could play jokes on each other and laugh about it.

After we were all done and the check was paid, everybody got up to leave.

McCarver reached over, grabbed the blazer on Filippelli's chair, and started to put it on.

They had switched seats before I got there.

I was mortified. I knew Tim well enough to know you did not prank him like that. He was big on leaving his stuff alone. As he put

---

23. I bet you didn't think I was a frat boy. . . . OK, I guess you probably did.

the coat on, he felt this bulge in the inside left pocket of his jacket, and said, "What the FUCK? I mean, God-DANG!"

He pulled out the napkin, and as he was unwrapping it, I jumped in and said, "Tim, I thought it was Flip's coat. I'm sorry. I'll buy you a new blazer."

To Tim's credit, he said, "It's fine. It's great." And he laughed. But I know inside he wanted to rip my head off, because that was just not a trick you play on Tim McCarver.

The coat was not ruined. I think he wore it in the playoffs for the next six years. But we rarely went to dinner together after that, and it's not because he was pissed. He wasn't. We just have different personalities. I was far more likely to go out to dinner with my *other* teammate in the booth, the one nobody ever saw.

Steve Horn doesn't appear on TV. I had used him as a resource only sporadically on the NFL. But when I got the baseball job, he called me and said, "I've covered baseball with Costas. It's kind of in my wheelhouse. I'd love to work with you and for you. Is that something you'd be interested in?"

I was definitely interested. I needed all the help I could get. I was in my midtwenties and would be doing the World Series on TV. I wanted safety nets under my safety nets. I didn't want to get four innings into my first game and realize I was comparing every situation to something that happened to the Louisville Redbirds. If Steve Horn was good enough for Costas, he was more than good enough for me.

Before long, Horn was off *FOX NFL Sunday* and working primarily with me. It's hard for outside people, even people at FOX, to understand what he does. The simple answer is that he makes me look good. And that ain't easy.

When I prepare for a game, I go through the notes provided by the teams, and stories provided by SportScan, a subscription service that sends me all the published stories about specific teams. I get a stats packet on the game I'm doing from STATS—the first four pages are team and league notes, and the next eight are individual notes on players. Then I lean on my own conversations with people in the sport, and all the information Horn gives me, the behind-the-scenes analysis that only he seems to know.

Steve looks like Tommy Lee Jones playing Joey Ramone in a movie. He has worn the same outfit since I met him: jeans, an Oxford shirt, a leather jacket, and black biker boots. I mean, in twenty years, he has not changed his wardrobe. He is the fashion industry's worst nightmare. His face hasn't changed much either. He is in his sixties but looks younger than fifty.

People sometimes ask if Horn gives me stats. That's like asking if Tom Brady is the guy who hands the ball to the tailback—he is, but that doesn't really capture his value. Anybody can look up statistics. I can have my nephew do that. Horn takes information and puts it together in a way that makes telecasts more interesting.

Horn grew up in St. Louis, but he went to Columbia and even drove a taxi in New York for a while. You don't see too many Columbia grads driving New York taxicabs. That's a pretty small demographic.

Horn gave me a New York sensibility. I felt I was always trying to please the New York critic. Whether it was Richard Sandomir of the *Times*, or Bob Raissman of the *Daily News*, or Phil Mushnick of the *Post* . . . I felt that, if you can pass their test, you pretty much can pass the test of the rest of the country. (Passing Rudy Martzke's test was also important, but for some reason, Martzke was a lot nicer to me than he was to my dad.)

Horn gives me a different point of view than the Midwest, conservative viewpoint that I would typically bring into something.

We meet all the time for lunch. He's kind of like my tutor. He'll ask me about the conflict in Bosnia and Herzegovina, and explain to me the workings and the history of that. Or he'll say certain Middle Eastern countries are basically corporations with flags, and that explains their interactions.

He has a smart way of looking at current events that I wouldn't have by just reading. He reads *The New York Times* every day. He highlights it and takes notes. He reads the front section and the arts or living section before he goes to the sports. But he can also tell me about the running style of Gale Sayers, or what made Sandy Koufax special, or what baseball was really like in the early 1960s. He has a way of contextualizing moments that might otherwise seem flat. When he sits next to me in the booth, I feel like I have the smartest guy in the room on my side. When I do football games, Horn has a headset and can talk directly to me.

One day in the midnineties, early in my FOX career, Horn asked me to go to lunch. When we sat down, he said:

"I'm going to tell you two things you're going to be mad about. You may not like me after this. But as your friend, as somebody who works with you, I feel like I need to tell you this. You can punch me in the face, or you can accept what I'm about to say."

Great. What is it? Do I suck?

He said, "First, you need to lose about thirty pounds, for two reasons. One, you're going to be on TV. Nobody likes looking at a fat guy on TV. Fat guys don't really exist on TV for the most part.

"Two, your dad is a type two diabetic. The lighter and thinner you can be, the more chance you have of fending that off. You're predisposed to all these things. You need to give yourself a fighting chance."

I decided not to punch him for that. He was right. It made sense. If you look at those tapes from 1995 and 1996, I am fat-faced. People want to see somebody on TV who is attractive, or at least not *unattractive*. And speaking of which . . .

Steve said, "And I think you need to look into getting hair plugs."

My hair?

"Funny you should say that," I said.

I told him I had already had some fresh sod laid down, and planned to continue the lawn maintenance in the future. So I didn't punch him for that, either.

You already know about my hair obsession. But I needed to think about my weight just as much. I am six-foot-one. I weighed 240 pounds at age nineteen, and if you weigh 240 at nineteen, you are in danger of weighing 340 at thirty-nine. Metabolisms do not magically improve as you get older. I am programmed to be chunky. Who knows what I would weigh right now if I hadn't started watching my diet? So I started to watch everything I ate, and I still do. Steve's comment was the best advice he ever gave me.

103

Chapter 7

Big Jumps

In the fall of 1996, I was twenty-seven and broadcasting my first World Series. The Yankees were playing the Braves, and the Yankees hosted Game 1. It's hard to capture just how mind-blowing that was. Yankee Stadium! The Yankees had not played in the World Series in fifteen years, which is an eternity for that franchise. Game 1 of the World Series at Yankee Stadium—it doesn't get much cooler than that.

Baseball has a different pace than football. When I arrive at a football game, all my prep work is done. I have four 11-by-17 pieces of cardboard full of info done by Saturday night at the latest. (I keep those boards in front of me throughout the game. They basically turn the game into an open-book test—all the info is there. I just have to find it.) By Sunday, if I could be assured of getting there five minutes before I went on TV, I could do that and be fine.

In baseball, I don't know the lineup or the defense until I arrive that day, usually about four hours before the game, because there are so many games and those things change day by day. For Game 1, I was slowing myself down, just trying to relax. Turns out, I relaxed too much. I fell behind, and then I had to scramble. I remember thinking, "My God, this game's going to start in an hour and I'm not even done. I don't even have all the regular season stats and postseason stats written in my scorebook!" It was like I was Captain Procrastination in high school again.

Eventually, the game got rained out. I was so happy. It pushed everything back a day. I could regroup. The baseball gods had smiled on me.

I arrived the next day at 3:00 P.M. for an 8:00 P.M. game. We talked to the managers and a few players. The rain delay had really helped me. I was so worried about being revealed as some fraud. *You're just somebody's kid. Who let you in the booth? Did you pick the lock?* I had a day to get that out of my system.

Thankfully, I had Tim with me, and broadcasting the World Series was routine for him by that point. He had seen and done just about anything that can happen on a baseball field.

The first two games went well, I thought, and the rainout also killed the travel day after Game 2. We flew to Atlanta that night, got in the next morning, and I was so keyed up that I couldn't sleep. I was supposed to take a nap but I couldn't do that, either. I got through it by taking my first hit of America's favorite drug: coffee. It was crappy

Fulton County Stadium press coffee. I had not moved up to Starbucks-level coffee addiction yet. But I would.

The rest of the World Series went well. I didn't step in any major puddles. It was a big moment for me, and I knew it, but I never thought about what I would say when the Yankees won the World Series, or when the Braves won the World Series. I try not to think like that. If you preplan your lines, they will sound preplanned. It does not work.

Yankees third baseman Charlie Hayes caught a foul ball to end Game 6 and win the World Series. "The Yankees are champions of baseball!" came out of my mouth. "Baseball is back in the Bronx!" That sounds strange now, because of how well the Yankees have done since then, but I think it was the right call at the time. People forget how frustrated Yankees fans were in the 1980s and early 1990s. A lot of their fans thought the glory days were over. They wanted George Steinbrenner to sell the team. Now they had won, and Wade Boggs was riding a police horse around Yankee Stadium, celebrating. That became the iconic image of that night, and none of us could have seen it coming.

At the end of the broadcast, the network wanted me to do a wrap-up monologue. Only six years had passed since I stood across town for a Cardinals broadcast with my earpiece on the floor and makeup dripping down my face. Now I was giving this little soliloquy into the camera after the Yankees won the World Series.

I had seen my dad do something similar for CBS at the end of the World Series. I remember I was kind of transfixed and nervous for him to get through it. Now I was doing it. I talked about Torre finally winning the World Series after decades in the big leagues. It was an emotional time for Joe—his oldest sibling, Rocco, had died that year, and his brother Frank, his idol, had gone through a heart transplant. I had known Torre my whole life, which made it easier for me.

I got through it. I called home. My dad answered.

I said, "Well, what did you think?"

And he said, "What did I think about what?"

"What did you think about the game?"

He said, "What time does it come on?"

Always the wiseass.

I said, "Shut up. You watched it."

He said, "It was great. It was great, Buck."

He handed the phone to my mom, and she went on and on and on, as many mothers do. My dad was very understated. That was just his way. He was extremely supportive of me, but he didn't give a ton of praise. Still, I was surprised he didn't say more. The next day, I called home again. My mom answered.

I said, "Why was Dad so short with me?"

She said, "He was crying so hard, he couldn't talk. He was just that proud."

Later that week, my mom and dad passed each other in their cars in our old neighborhood. One was going home, and the other was going out. They stopped and looked at each other like, "How great was that? Our son just did the World Series!" But they didn't say anything. They just kind of looked at each other, nodded, and drove on.

A few years earlier, I had watched my father do games with Tim and winced. Now my dad was watching me do games with Tim and he was smiling. My on-air chemistry with Tim was great.

Early in my time with McCarver, my goal every Saturday, when we broadcast our regular *Game of the Week* to a national TV audience, was to make him laugh. FOX's *Game of the Week* was an even bigger deal then than it is now—we had exclusive Saturday windows with no other games, and there weren't nearly as many channels as there are today. But we were still doing regular-season baseball games. I wanted the broadcast to be fun. Tim has a great sense of humor, and a great laugh, and I wanted people to hear it.

Chemistry and delivery are so important when you try to be funny. We shared the postseason with NBC; they had Bob Uecker, who is probably the most naturally funny man ever to be in sports. He is certainly way funnier than I am. But Joe Morgan was in the booth with him along with Bob Costas, and Morgan didn't really laugh at Uecker's jokes, which made it kind of weird. Tim and I would genuinely laugh with each other.

Horn would tell me, "I hope you realize how great an audience you have in Tim." I did. He gave me instant credibility and was the kind of audience for me that he never was for my dad.

I selfishly wanted him to be there with me because he was the ultimate security blanket. Nothing could happen in 1996 that he hadn't witnessed before. And I think he realized FOX was invested in me in a way that CBS had never been invested in my father. Even though I was much younger than Tim, I had actually worked for FOX longer than he had.

But it was more than just power plays. It was a genuine friendship. We hit it off.

Tim worked so hard. He never acted like he knew the game better than anybody because he'd played it. He read. He talked to players. He talked to managers. He was critical. He had foresight. He wasn't looking back. I think, at his peak, he was the best baseball analyst to ever do TV, because he wasn't worried about upsetting somebody. If he did tick somebody off, he'd walk right into the clubhouse the next day and face him. He really was the complete package. He made my job so much easier for a lot of years, and he was the ultimate partner for me. I used to kid him that he was like an older brother to me—a much, *much* older brother.

When FOX started to acquire major sports properties, a lot of fans worried that FOX didn't give a shit about sports. The truth: FOX doesn't give a shit about critics. And that attitude helped revolutionize TV sports broadcasting.

Sure, I'm biased. But FOX was willing to try stuff nobody else would even consider—and if it didn't work, FOX would just abandon it and move on.

It usually worked. FOX was the first network to put the score and time of an NFL game in the corner of the screen. We call it the FOX Box. A lot of people, including NBC's Dick Ebersol, said it was foolish—they said viewers would flip the channel to that game, see the score, and then keep flipping. That's like saying, "Let's keep the viewer hostage by hiding the score." Now everybody has the score up there. You would get ridiculed if you *didn't* do it.

FOX put microphones in bases, in foul poles, in outfield walls, and on football officials, so you can hear the snap count and pads crunching. FOX put lipstick-shaped cameras in front of home plate. That stuff is TV magic. FOX put a little balloon and arrows on the screen during NASCAR broadcasts to tell you which car was which.

Yeah, FOX also had that glowing hockey puck in the 1990s, which turned a lot of people off. I love hockey. I think the glowing puck was ahead of its time—the idea was solid, but the technology wasn't there yet. If you were doing it now, in high-definition, you could make the puck stand out without looking silly.

FOX has tried to put a camera on a pulley system over a baseball diamond, like we have in football, but Major League Baseball is worried about fly balls hitting cameras. We put cameras on drones for golf. We put microphones in the golf holes, allowing us to pick up conversations between players. It's one cutting-edge move after another.

I don't want to sound like I'm taking *any* credit at all for any of this. These are rarely my ideas. (I have lobbied to interview batters in the on-deck circle during an All-Star Game, and I would love to talk to a center fielder during game action, but nobody has gone for that. Yet.) I'm just thankful to work at a place that takes viewers where they haven't been before. It's fun to be a part of it.

Occasionally, we also take the broadcaster to a place *he* has never been before. Sometimes that works out, and sometimes it doesn't.

In 1998, David Hill asked me if I would do a live motorcycle jump in Las Vegas. The good news was I would not be the one on the motorcycle. I just had to talk about it. The guy on the motorcycle was Robbie Knievel, Evel's son.

Our show was called *Daredevils Live: Shattering the Records*. I thought it would be a dramatic event. There was a lot to like: It's live, it's network TV, and this guy is defying death by jumping over thirty limousines. I'm old enough to remember Evel Knievel and those jumps in the Snake River Canyon. Evel had a much heavier motorcycle, so he couldn't jump as far.

Robbie signed this deal with FOX, and he was going to get a ton of money to do this jump. I got to know Robbie a little bit. He was extremely nice. As we prepared for the broadcast, I was strongly in favor of him not getting killed.

The day before the jump, Robbie was out there doing dry runs: taking his bike up to the top of the ramp that his guys were building, and gunning it. The thirty limos were all in place, but he wasn't going to jump over them that night. He was just getting a feel for the ramp.

Well, Evel came out and started talking to him. The talk became an argument between father and son. It was getting heated. I was doing rehearsals with Ron Pitts, who was doing the broadcast with me. We had a two-hour show and a jump that would take less than a minute, so it was tricky. We really had to sell the whole death-defying nature of it to the audience: *If he hits that last limousine, this is what his spleen will look like!*

Evel and Robbie kept arguing. They were getting animated. Finally, I watched Robbie take his bike up to the top of the ramp.

He gunned it down the ramp and took off, into the air, over the limos.

Our cameras were not on. There was no money at stake for him. FOX was paying him to land the jump on national television, not in practice. I was stunned. And then, *as his motorcycle was flying through the air*, Robbie took one hand off the handlebar and gave his father the finger. Then he put his hand back on the handlebar, landed the jump, and went inside. That was the end of his warm-up.

I looked at Ron Pitts and said: "Did that just happen?"

And so the whole next night, we were sitting on TV acting like Robbie Knievel was defying death, but I knew Robbie was not the least bit worried about landing the jump. He had done it the day before, just as a fuck-you to his dad.

In 1999, David Hill had another idea. He asked me to do a live bass-fishing broadcast. Those words—*live bass-fishing broadcast*—should never appear in that order. Our show was a disaster. I would have preferred to be one of the fish.

First of all, those bass-fishing guys weren't used to doing live broadcasts. There were some technical hurdles. Obviously, you're not going to have cables going to their boats. It was all on radio frequency, with wireless earpieces and microphones. I was supposed to interview these guys while they were on these different lakes in the Orlando area, pulling in different fish.

FOX asked me, "What do you know about fishing?"

I said, "I had a fish tank in college. That's about it. I know how to clean a fish tank. I don't know anything about bass fishing, lures, boats, any of it."

They said, "Perfect! You're hired."

I don't know what answer would have gotten me out of it. Maybe if I said my favorite fish was Swedish fish, or the one on *Barney Miller*.

I had already done a World Series. I had no burning desire to do a bass-fishing tournament, and I felt I had earned the right to turn it down. But David said, "This is going to be the next fucking NASCAR. We're going to see the fish hit the line!"

In other words: "Please?"

He was asking me for a favor. I said yes because it was David Hill. I'd do anything for David Hill.

There were three of us in a studio on this lakeshore: former major-league catcher Bob Brenly, who was a big outdoorsman; Forrest L. Wood, who is the creator of the modern-day bass-fishing boat; and me, who kept a fish named Oscar alive for a little while in college.

The show was ninety minutes long. If it had been ninety-one minutes, we would have had a minute of dead air because I had prepared exactly ninety minutes of material on everything from the history of the bass boat to who the fishermen were. I was tapped.

So if you ask me, "Joe, what's the dumbest thing you ever said on the air?" it would be anything I said during those ninety minutes.

I was up there saying, "Obviously, these guys are trying to catch fish . . . the bigger, the better." I can imagine what the fourteen people who were watching thought of that. *Oh, so they want to catch BIGGER fish? Is that what you're saying? It's not a contest to catch the SMALLEST fish? Bigger is better? Thanks, Sherlock.*

Some of these competing gladiators forgot to turn their microphones on when they were out on a lake, and so as I was trying to talk to them from the studio desk, they were talking into a dead microphone. I couldn't hear anything they were saying. If they gave out an Emmy for Worst 90 Minutes of Television, we would have won, then dropped the trophy.

The big finale, the big payoff, the moment that would turn bass fishing into the next fucking NASCAR was supposed to be . . . weighing the fish. Exciting, huh? It was like a weigh-in for a boxing title match, except instead of humans we used fish, and also there was no fight.

And we couldn't even do *that* right. They were putting these fish up and the weights were wrong. It was such a debacle.

I don't remember if I asked David Hill what he thought of our broadcast. I didn't need to hear him say, "Shitty," in his Australian accent. The good news: Nobody ever asked me to broadcast bass fishing again.

Except for that unfortunate bass-fishing interlude, my career was going better than I could have dreamed. So was my life. In the mid-1990s, thanks to my FOX contract, Ann and I were able to buy a bigger house. It was almost 4,000 square feet, much bigger than the house I grew up in.

My father walked in and said, "Who the hell is going to live with you—the Rams?" They had just moved to St. Louis.

I showed him around. After he had seen most of the house, I said, "Dad, there's a third floor."

He said, "I'm sure it's great."

He never walked up there. Ever. He just said, "The house is too big."

I didn't think it was too big. But my world was getting bigger by the day. One day, Ann bounded up the steps of our house and said, "You are on the Monica Lewinsky tapes!" That was weird. I had no recollection of meeting Monica. I was ready to tell my wife I did not have sexual relations with that woman when I learned that, while Lewinsky was spilling secrets to Linda Tripp, you could hear my voice in the background, plain as day: "*Ground ball to Jeter . . .*"

It's strange, but moments like that are when you realize how far sports reach. When you're at the stadium, doing a game, you just think about the game. You don't really think that the president might be watching. Or his intern.

We were happy in our house, and with our lives. But I wouldn't say we were ever *content*, and that's a big difference. In 1996, we joined Old Warson Country Club, which was a real treat for me because I am obsessed with the game of golf. And sometimes I would go to the course and think, "Man, what if we could live right here, next to the course? That would be so great." There we were, living in this beautiful 4,000-square-foot house that my dad said was too big, and I was already thinking about upgrading.

When I was born, in Florida, my dad was calling a Cardinals game in Philadelphia. When my mom called to tell him the news, he said, "Thank you." She can still remember the sweetness in his voice. It was a pretty strong turnaround from when she told him she was pregnant and he said his knees were melting into the pavement.

But my dad never considered skipping work to see my birth. There were balls and strikes to call. That's just how his generation operated. In the 1960s and 1970s, fathers were not expected to be in the delivery room or change diapers. I don't think my father even hugged us until we were potty-trained.[24]

The world had changed by June 7, 1996, when Ann gave birth to our first child, Natalie. It was now accepted for a player to miss a game to be there for the birth of his child. And if players could skip work, an announcer sure could, too. Those balls and strikes are still balls and strikes, no matter who calls them.

The Cardinals found a familiar voice to replace me on their West Coast swing: my dad. He had stopped traveling with the team at that point, for the most part—he stuck to home games. But he went to the West Coast so I could be with Ann. This was the one and only time anybody could say he got a job because of me.

I was so giddy when Natalie was born, I called my dad at around 4:00 A.M. Pacific time, never even thinking he might be asleep. I was bawling and could barely squeak the words out. He was so happy on the other end. I could hear it in his voice. It was a moment I will never forget.

We did not know we were having a girl until Natalie was born, and Ann had literally just finished pushing and I was in her ear, asking if she thought the next one would be a boy.

I was in Boston preparing for the 1999 baseball All-Star Game when Ann was days away from delivering Mystery Child number two.

---

24. That was a joke.

If I got the call that she was in labor, I was going to fly home immediately and let somebody else take over. We had a whole plan in place. I don't remember who would pick up the play-by-play if I left, but it wouldn't have been a problem. You couldn't swing a dead cat in Fenway Park without hitting six play-by-play guys.

I thought we would be OK because when Natalie was born, we had to induce—it seemed unlikely that number two would take the express train. Still, it was a bit stressful, wondering if the call was going to come as Pedro Martinez pitched the first inning.

That's a called strike two and . . . whoops! I gotta go, everybody!

That All-Star Game featured one of the most moving pregame ceremonies I've ever witnessed. Ted Williams made both his triumphant return and his grand exit—all in one trip, from the right-field corner to home plate.

The ovation was thunderous. Williams always had a complicated relationship with the public and with Boston, but in that moment, he was truly touched. As he took off his hat and saluted the fans, I was silent. Our producer, the great Mike Weisman, shouted into my ear: "We are on! Go, Joe! We are on!"

I tried to speak, but nothing would come out. I was so choked with emotion that I was scared my voice would squeak. That would ruin the moment for viewers. Imagine millions of people wiping away a tear and then saying, "Hey, did Joe Buck just hit puberty?"

It was best for everybody that I didn't and couldn't talk. The emotion of the moment was there for anyone at home to feel, the same way it was for any lucky fan with a ticket that night. It was one of the best calls I never made.

Ted threw the ceremonial first pitch from a cart. San Diego Padres star Tony Gwynn, a close friend and kindred batting spirit of Williams, caught it. We were supposed to go to a commercial, but Weisman sensed something special was about to happen and decided to stay on air—defying his boss, who was sitting behind him.

Then Gwynn and the other current players in the game all walked up to Ted's cart and gathered around it, just to be close to him. You could see how much he meant to them—and that Williams still watched and cared about the game he had dominated.

It was extraordinary television, and we got it because Weisman refused to go to commercial. We got to hear Ted ask Mark McGwire if he ever smelled smoke when he fouled a ball off his bat. Having that on tape would have been nice. Having it *live* was great.

Two days later, Ann gave birth to another girl. We named her Trudy. We never did have a son, and I never cared. My girls are my life.

Chapter 8

Thrills and Chills
(and Steroids)

During the 1997 season, the Cardinals traded for a new first baseman—a guy who had been injured a lot but was one of the best power hitters in baseball when he was healthy. We didn't realize it at the time, but he would quickly become the biggest story in all of sports. His name, of course, was Mark McGwire.

McGwire was a quiet guy, and he didn't easily blend into a clubhouse full of major-league players. It was one reason the Cardinals kept second baseman Pat Kelly around. He was a buddy of McGwire's.

Mark had an appreciation for baseball history, and for people who had contributed to the game. And he took to my dad instantly. My father's health was starting to deteriorate—he had been diagnosed with Parkinson's disease—but he was still doing Cardinals games, and Mark loved him.

In early August 1998, the Cardinals played a series in Atlanta. I was doing a national game for FOX that weekend, so I wasn't with the Cardinals. I caught up to the team in Milwaukee and met Mark at a bar near the Pfister Hotel.

Mark had a story he couldn't wait to tell me.

While the team was in Atlanta, Mark and a friend went to a strip joint downtown called the Cheetah Club. The bouncer came up to him in the VIP room and said, "Mark, there's some old dude down there, some white-haired guy, says he knows you, says he's with the Cardinals and he wants to come up."

Mark said: "No way . . . Jack Buck! Hell yeah! Bring him up."

He said my dad came in and started telling jokes. He had the strippers laughing so hard.

Three weeks later, the Cardinals dedicated a statue of my dad. They placed it in front of the old Busch Stadium. (They hadn't moved to the new one yet.) It was a beautiful tribute, and it was another sign that my father was in the late innings of his career. The year before, he had published his autobiography. It was called *Jack Buck: That's a Winner*. When I read the first chapter of the manuscript, I didn't think it sounded like him. So I rewrote the chapter for him.

But in front of a microphone, he was so good at finding the right words. As the Cardinals honored him at home plate, he stood up there, shaking with Parkinson's, and said:

"I've given the Cardinals the best years of my life . . . and now I'm going to give them the worst."

McGwire was off to the side, calling my dad Cheetah. He kept yelling, "Cheetah! Cheetah!"[25]

Mark is a very private person. When we were on charters together, I'd talk to him for the majority of the flight. He had just gotten divorced, and we would talk about that, or other stuff that had very little to do with baseball. He would chew on the cap of a water bottle until it was flat. Other players left him alone.

He'd ask me, "Oh, what game are you doing this week on FOX? Let me guess: Yankees–Red Sox."

I'd say, "Yeah. Yankees–Red Sox."

He would ask why those teams were always on FOX, and I'd say, "Let me tell you why: because people watch." Is there an East Coast bias? Absolutely, there is. Networks are biased toward getting viewers.

McGwire was one of the first people to give me crap for all those Yankees and Red Sox games on FOX. And the funny thing was that I don't think he really enjoyed being on national TV himself. He didn't like being near the spotlight at all. But he wouldn't be able to avoid it in 1998.

It was clear, from the start of the 1998 season, that McGwire was chasing history. He hit home runs in each of the Cardinals' first four games. In one game in mid-April, he hit three. In one game in mid-May, he hit three again. By the end of May, he had 27.

---

25. The next year, when I was in Houston with the Cardinals, one player said, "You got to go to Rick's strip joint. We were there last night. Pay attention to the pictures on the wall going to the bathroom." There was a picture of my father there. Nice work, Dad. You're in at least one Strip Club Hall of Fame.

As every American sports fan knew, the single-season record was 61, hit by Roger Maris in 1961. It might have been the most hallowed record in sports. McGwire had hit 58 the year before, and now he was hitting them at an even faster pace. The chase was on.

Fans came out in droves just to watch Mark take batting practice, which baffled him. He didn't understand the fuss. One time, in Montreal, he stepped to the plate for BP and started hitting balls where balls had never been hit before in Olympic Stadium. The fans there were oohing and aahing and whistling—that shrill whistling they do when they see something amazing.

He turned to me and said, "What are they . . ."

I said, "Mark, nobody sees this. It's a freak show, and you're providing it."

The same thing happened at Dodger Stadium. Mark went to USC. They loved him in California. When he would get in the cage, they always played the Fatboy Slim song "Praise You." Mark was hitting these bombs in batting practice, and for a lot of paying customers, that show was as good as the game.

But he didn't like it. He would be out to eat and somebody would interrupt him mid-bite. He hated that. And yet, he would get to the ballpark, with all eyes on him, and continually do one of the toughest things in sports: crush major-league pitching.

It was an incredible thing to watch up close every day. Adding to the thrill: Even though Maris set the record as a Yankee, he also played for the Cardinals, and was one of Mike Shannon's best friends. My dad had befriended him as well. I had met Maris a couple of times in my dad's radio booth after he retired. Maris was just hanging out.

So when McGwire chased Maris's record of 61 home runs, it was history for the big world of baseball, but also a really cool moment in our smaller world: a Cardinal we knew, chasing a former Cardinal that my father knew. Maris had died in 1985, so there weren't many people who really knew both him and McGwire well. But my dad did.

As it turned out, McGwire's biggest competition for the single-season title was not even Maris but a power hitter from the Chicago Cubs, Sammy Sosa. They went back and forth all summer, but by early September, you could see that McGwire would break the record first. And in a serendipitous bit of scheduling, he was sitting on 60 home runs when Sosa's Cubs visited St. Louis.

McGwire hit a home run on Monday night to tie Maris at 61. The next night, Ed Goren and David Hill got FOX to bump all the prime-time programming so we could show McGwire's attempt to hit number 62. That was incredible: bumping prime-time programming for a regular-season baseball game. But in 1998, it was the right call.

McGwire tried to limit his media sessions because he was so uncomfortable talking about himself. But that night, I got to do a sit-down interview with Sosa and McGwire together. I interviewed both of them, ping-ponging back and forth. It was less than three hours before first pitch. If he had been Mark McGwire of the Atlanta Braves, I might not have gotten that interview. But through all of our time together with the Cardinals, we had become friends.

They got up at the end of the interview. Sosa was the first one to walk out. McGwire was trailing him. Mark came up to me and said:

"Better be ready to make the call tonight. It's happening."

It's happening.

That was not in character for him. Some guys talk trash in their sleep. McGwire *never* did it. All year, he kept saying he was just trying to play baseball. I was stunned. Thinking about that gives me chills, even today.

I was twenty-nine years old, and I already knew McGwire was right: I had to be ready. All summer, because I did Cardinals games, people were asking me, "What are you going to say when he breaks the record?"

I'd say, "Whatever strikes me."

I wasn't being coy. That's just not how I do the job. But then somebody else would ask me. And somebody else. He got to 50 home runs. More people asked me. Then he got to 55. And more people asked.

I still wasn't thinking about it. Then he got to the high 50s, and people were saying, "Well, it could happen next week. *What are you going to say, Joe?*"

And then my bosses at FOX moved their whole night of programming to make this a national TV game.

Suddenly, winging it did not seem like a good idea. I went to bed thinking about what I was going to say. I woke up thinking about it. I finally came up with something. I wrote this little script in my scorebook: *McGwire around the bases, and into the history books!*

McGwire stepped in for his second plate appearance of the game in the fourth inning. All of his home runs had seemed like missile launchings—when the ball left the bat, you just wondered which deck it would puncture. I was ready for another moon shot.

This time, there was no moon shot. McGwire hit this screaming line drive toward left field. It hooked down into the corner. Could have been a homer. Could have been off the wall for a double. Could have been foul. I was standing one booth to the right from my normal spot with the Cardinals, in the national booth, so I had a better angle on that scorcher into the left-field corner than I normally would.

I could see it *barely* get over and *barely* stay fair for number 62.

I had to keep my head up and make sure that it was gone before I called it. So I didn't even have a chance to look down to read the stupid script I wrote.

Instead, I said: "Down the left-field line . . . is it enough? *Gone! There it is!*"

Sosa was in right field, clapping. And because I kept my head up, instead of looking at this script, I saw that McGwire was so excited, he missed first base on his home-run trot. He had to go back. This gave me an opening:

"Touch first, Mark! You are the new single-season home-run king!"

I think it worked because it was so obviously *not* scripted. I had no idea McGwire would miss first base. And I stopped talking after that for around three minutes, while McGwire picked up his kids, hugged his teammates, and even hugged Sosa, who ran in from right field to congratulate him. Then he went into the stands and hugged Maris's family. It was one of the greatest lessons I've ever had in my career. I learned to trust myself. Trust what I see. Don't write some cheesy script beforehand. That's not what makes sports fun.

After the game, Mark was trying to set another record: for hugs. He had already hugged damn near everybody in the stadium, including groundskeepers and guys *on the opposing team*, the Cubs, who were in a pennant race. He had his family on the field with him. I was there to interview him. He hugged everybody in his family, and I was standing there.

So he hugged me.

I got some grief for it. I understand. But I didn't feel like I could say, "Hey, no! Don't hug me! I'm the broadcaster guy!" It was just a mutual thing because he was a buddy.

It crossed the line, and it was a mistake. But when it was going on, it didn't feel weird. I liked him and I admired him. I was appreciative of what he had done for me that whole year, him bothering to sit down and do that interview. I found him to be a great guy.

McGwire had caught Maris, but he still had to fend off Sosa. He did it, finishing with 70 home runs, including two on the last day. (Sosa finished with 66.) I did the game where he hit number 70 for FOX Midwest. Incredible. All those years, people said nobody would ever hit 62 home runs, and this guy hit *70*.

It almost didn't feel real. Some people would argue it wasn't.

Mark McGwire took performance-enhancing drugs. You are probably aware of this. He admitted it, and by the time he admitted it, most Americans assumed it was true anyway. It has probably kept him out of the Hall of Fame.

A lot of people have said that the media all knew he was on steroids back then, and we turned a blind eye toward it. I think that's revisionist history. During McGwire's home-run chase in 1998, Steve Wilstein, a reporter for the Associated Press, reported that McGwire kept androstenedione in his locker. So somebody did report it, but most of us had no concept of the scope of what was happening. I'd never heard of andro. The next thing I knew, I was doing an interview about it with Shepard Smith on FOX News. But it still didn't seem like a smoking gun to me.

There were suspicions that some guys might have been on steroids, but that dated back to the eighties, if not the seventies.

Whitey Herzog had a theory that makes a lot of sense: Steroids got into baseball when all the multipurpose stadiums were built. The football Cardinals were working out with the baseball Cardinals. The Raiders were working out with the A's, the Steelers with the Pirates, the Reds with the Bengals. They were sharing weight rooms. The facilities weren't what they are now. The football guys would show up, and the baseball guys would look at them and say, "Wow, how did you get so big?" Steroids were all over the NFL then. So it's logical that it would go from one sport to the other.

Who knows when it started? If you think that *no* players from the seventies and eighties did steroids, that is naïve at best. It would not surprise me if a Hall of Famer or two from that era used performance enhancers.

So were there rumblings about steroids in 1998? Absolutely. Was McGwire one name on a long list of suspects? No doubt about it.

Were reporters standing in a big circle in the clubhouse, watching McGwire get injected with steroids?

Hell no.

When Mark was hitting all those home runs, I guess I had a vague sense that he *might* be on steroids, but I really didn't give it a lot of thought. Apparently, I was not alone, because most of the media and most of the country celebrated his achievement without reservation.

Eventually, Ken Caminiti revealed he took steroids when he won the National League MVP, and Jose Canseco wrote his tell-all book, and we heard more about Barry Bonds, Roger Clemens, Sosa, McGwire, and others. I thought about it more. When Mark told a congressional committee that he was "not here to talk about the past," it was pretty obvious. I mean, if your wife accused you of cheating on you, and you were innocent, you wouldn't say, "I'm not here to talk about the past." You'd swear from here to China that you were faithful.

He had obviously lawyered up—and lawyered up very poorly. He didn't want to perjure himself, but at the same time, he should have said more. Remember, Mark was uncomfortable with *positive* attention. You can imagine how uncomfortable he was as he testified before Congress. But he should have just told the whole truth, and I think he would have seemed human.

Knowing what we know now, it's easy to rip the media in the nineties, including me. But back then, what did we really know? I mean, what are you supposed to say as an announcer? *What a home run! Look at the muscles on this guy! Makes you wonder if he is on steroids, doesn't it? And the Cardinals lead, 6–2, with two outs in the sixth . . .*

It's easy for people to say *now*, "You're supposed to be the one to stand up and call it all a farce."

Well, first of all, it still doesn't feel like a farce to me. This is just my opinion. But for as many guys as there were hitting home runs juiced up on steroids, there were plenty of pitchers on the mound equally juiced up. It was all relative to the era.

Do McGwire's 70 home runs denigrate the record book? Yeah. But it happened because the stuff became available to these guys. I don't think that the guys in the sixties and fifties were better human beings and wouldn't have taken it. They just never had the opportunity to take performance-enhancing drugs.

Or I should say: They never had the opportunity to take *those* drugs. They could take greenies, which are amphetamines. Those were used a lot in the years before anybody ever heard of Mark McGwire, and to me, a greenie is as much a performance-enhancing drug as steroids.

There is no doubt that the drugs gave him more power. But I think the biggest advantage was being able to physically recover every day. I am personally convinced that these guys are led to taking some sort of performance-enhancing supplement because of the schedule. Sometimes they play thirty-six games in thirty-seven days. I just don't know how a body does that. The performance enhancers get them off the trainer's table more than turning a 390-foot home run into a 500-foot home run.

I know Mark said the steroids didn't help him hit home runs. My response is: "Well, they *did* help you hit home runs because they got you off the trainer's table and into the lineup every day. You can't hit home runs if you can't play."

This is a long way of saying that when I look back on 1998, I still love that season. I know it's not a popular stance. I know more about what was going on than I did then, but it still doesn't take the fun away from it for me. And it was fun for a few reasons:

1. It was this historic chase that nobody thought would happen. People thought the media scrutiny would be too much

for any hitter to keep going, and we wouldn't see anybody break the record in this lifetime. That was the conventional wisdom for many years. That proved to be wrong.

2. I got to ride alongside my dad, watching this chase. On the road, we would go to the ballpark together, then split up when the game started—him in the radio booth, me doing TV. McGwire's 62nd home run surpassed all those great moments he broadcast when I was a kid, and I got to do it *with* him. My dad loved Mark—and every minute of the drama of 1998. Those moments energized him, and his calls reflected that.

3. I liked the guy who broke the record. I still do. I'm not going to demonize him for taking steroids.

I know that, as a sports announcer, I'm supposed to hyperventilate and shake with anger at athletes who put something in their bodies to "enhance their performance." I just can't bring myself to do it. And maybe I'm wrong, but on a daily basis, I don't think fans are that upset or worried about it.

Baseball is as popular and profitable as it's ever been. For all of the supposed "outrage" by fans, they rarely turn their backs on their own players. They throw inflatable needles and yell nasty things at *opposing* players who have been caught. That's just gamesmanship. Fans cheer when those guys are on their team. The bottom line is that fans haven't really walked away from sports because of steroid use.

McGwire was wrong to do what he did. But he didn't do anything out of malice. Deep down, Mark wanted to play, and wanted to play well. He was not chasing fame or money. He hated all the trappings that went with being Mark McGwire. I think that's why he walked away when he did.

People forget this, but he walked away from $30 million at the end of his career. He had it coming to him. All he had to do was not retire. He didn't even have to play. He could have been a batting-practice draw and an occasional pinch hitter, or he could have been released and he still would have gotten that $30 million. After all the money Mark had made for the Cardinals, that $30 million was change under the couch cushions to them. But he chose to walk away from the money. That's admirable. I mean, if you're going to talk about the bad stuff a guy did, talk about the good, too.

McGwire's "once-in-a-lifetime" achievement did not last very long. In 2001, Barry Bonds hit 73 home runs. That didn't feel the same to most of America, because the record was only three years old, and also because he was Barry Bonds.

McGwire didn't like attention. Bonds seemed as if he didn't even like people. I had experienced this firsthand. In the early nineties, I was chatting with Don Baylor, the Cardinals hitting coach, before a game against Pittsburgh. I would get to the ballpark really early and I would sit in the dugout and talk about hitting and life with Baylor. It was a wonderful education. Baylor is such a great guy.

We were in the dugout, watching the Pirates take batting practice. Bonds was with Pittsburgh at the time, and he was putting on a show in BP. Bonds was young, but he had already shown he was an all-time great player, and also a jerk. At least, that was my take on it.

I shared my view with Don. I said, "The guy is so good, so much better than everyone else, and he just seems to hate being here. He's such a surly prick."

Baylor said, "Barry? C'mon."

I said, "Yes. Barry Bonds. He stares right through you."

He said, "Come here."

Baylor grabbed my hand and walked me to the batting cage. Bonds finished his batting practice. He saw Don and gave him this big hug, like you might give an old buddy.

Don said, "Hey, I want you to meet a friend of mine. This is Joe Buck. He's one of our broadcasters. He's the son of another one of our broadcasters, Jack Buck."

Barry leaned back. He looked at me, and looked at Don, and said: "So?"

That was it. He didn't shake my hand. He didn't say anything else. Don and I walked back to the dugout.

I said, "As I was saying . . ."

Baylor said, "Wow, that was unbelievable."

I said, "Well, there you go."

It was a bad moment for me, because it proved what you sometimes suspect as a media member: A lot of these guys want nothing to do with you. But over time, I have learned: If they don't want to talk to me, so what? I'm not going to beg. Enough guys will talk. You still do your job.

Most of the time, a guy with Bonds's attitude is not going to give you anything anyway. So we don't grab the guy kicking and screaming into our production meeting or an interview, because it's a waste of time. We can't waterboard guys until they tell us which pitches they like to hit.

And then there are players who desperately care what you think. That can be strange, too. I remember when Ken Griffey Jr. played for the Mariners, and he was the most popular player in baseball, for good reason. He had his hat on backward during batting practice, he always had this huge smile, and he looked like he was having the time of his life. He was playing a kid's game for a living. He knew it and he loved it.

Then, in 2000, he got traded (at his request) to Cincinnati, his hometown. And that kid—his nickname actually was the Kid—seemed worn out. He had battled injuries in Cincinnati and was never the same player he had been in Seattle. Some fans turned on him.

On a Cardinals-Reds broadcast one night, I said, "You know, Griffey was the most marketable guy for a reason, because he was lovable when he was with Seattle. And now it just looks like he's not having any fun playing baseball anymore."

I didn't say much more than that. It seemed like a mild criticism. I certainly didn't expect what happened the next day.

Griffey was around the cage for batting practice. He walked up to Mike Shannon and asked, "Which one of these guys is Joe Buck?" Shannon directed him toward me.

Griffey was looking at me, talking to people on the team, and looking back at me. I could tell that he wanted to say something.

But he still wouldn't come up to me.

Finally, I went to Griffey and said, "Is there something you want to say to me?"

He said, "Yeah, I got something I want to say to you. My wife was listening to the Cardinals' broadcast last night, because the Reds broadcasters hate me. She can't listen to them. You said that it doesn't look like I have any fun playing this game."

I said, "That's just what it looks like to *me*, as an outsider. I don't know you. I'm just talking about how you looked when you were with Seattle and how you look now."

He said, "Well, how can you say that?"

I said, "It's just an observation."

He said, "Well, let me tell you why I'm not having any fun. I got traded to my hometown. People don't want me there. I get death threats."

He went on and on and on.

I said, "That's why I said what I said."

So he was mad I said he wasn't having fun, then he started telling me *why* he wasn't having fun. I guess that can happen when a guy isn't having fun.

We talked it over and moved on to other topics. Then, at the end of the conversation, he said, "All right, I'll put on a smile for you tonight."

I said, "OK."

I thought he was joking. But then the game started, and soon the PA announcer said: "*Now batting for the Reds . . . Ken Griffey Jr.!*" and I looked down.

Griffey walked from the on-deck circle to home plate, stopped halfway, and looked up at our booth. Then he gave this huge, wide, fake-ass grin, as if to say: "Look at me, I'm smiling!" Then he put his head down, walked in, and went to the plate.

It was weird, but it was also funny and kind of endearing. Here was one of the best players of the last fifty years openly admitting that words could hurt him.

Chapter 9

We Are Blessed

I was lucky that my rise to prominence in baseball broadcasting coincided with the revitalization of the Yankees. They were considered dysfunctional for most of the eighties and early nineties, but starting in 1996, they went on one of the great runs in baseball history. That was my rookie year on FOX's MLB coverage, the year I'd been so excited to broadcast the World Series, and it was Derek Jeter's rookie year with the Yankees.

I would do more of Jeter's games than of any non-Cardinal over the years. He was always professional with us, but I never got to know him that well. That was part of Jeter's persona, and maybe part of his success—he never got too close to the media.

Before his last All-Star Game, in Minnesota in 2014, we had some fun with this. I walked into the American League clubhouse, said hi to Miguel Cabrera on camera, walked past Mike Trout and mentioned him, then got to Jeter.

Jeter said: "Get out of here. We've got a game to play."

I thought it was funny—anybody can show a live television interview, but who shows getting *rejected* for an interview? And Jeter was in on the joke. He was sort of winking at his own reputation for keeping the media at arm's length.

Some people online said, "That was awesome. Jeter just showed up Joe Buck." Showed me up? I wrote it! Some people just don't get that stuff. They thought he was serious.

Jeter and I were never close. But of all the baseball players that I've ever covered, I think Jeter was the best all-around package. When you look at what he did, where he did it, and how he did it . . . it's astounding. It became vogue in the last few years to say Jeter was overrated. I think it's just our society and our nature now to tear guys down like that.

Keith Olbermann, a lifelong Yankees fan, did this whole rant toward the end of Jeter's career about how overrated he was. Stupid. Jeter was the captain of a Yankee team in a much more intensely scrutinized world, and if the bases were loaded and you had a one-run lead in the ninth inning, you'd want the screaming shot hit at him. He'd make the play. He was a clutch player, however you define *clutch*. He didn't hit a home run in every big moment, but he handled those moments as well as anyone.

He also did it in New York. He didn't make a lot of missteps. Babe Ruth and Mickey Mantle could get drunk and carouse and nobody wrote about it. Jeter played in an age when people were *dying* to write about that stuff, but he rarely waded into controversy. He could be distant, but he was respectful. I've never been more impressed with a player talking into a microphone than when George Steinbrenner died during the All-Star break and Jeter took the mic when the Yankees returned home and talked from the heart as his career was winding down.

I got a little frustrated with Jeter because I think he always had a little bit more to give—not on the field, but with his personality. I think he was just so programmed to not reveal anything that he became a boring quote. That was probably for self-preservation, which was totally understandable but kind of a shame. When you watched him talk about Steinbrenner that day, you realized there was more there, a guy who could talk so eloquently. It's hard to stand there and talk from the heart in front of a crowd like that.

Was he Babe Ruth? No. Was he Ozzie Smith at shortstop? No. But he was a great player, and he had a presence that really helped those teams thrive in New York. Do you think Joe Torre thought he was overrated? Jeter and Mariano Rivera controlled that Yankees clubhouse. Think of all the controversies that could have derailed the team and didn't. I just think people don't get what Jeter meant to the Yankees and to the game.

My dad was sixty-seven years old when CBS fired him from its number one baseball team in 1991. That is, of course, a reasonable retirement age, even for a man who counted every penny he had. I didn't really expect him to retire, but I did urge him to ease off a bit. I wanted him to enjoy the rest of his life and appreciate everything he had done in his career.

He didn't see it that way. He kept doing Cardinals games and *Monday Night Football* on the radio. He had Parkinson's and diabetes, but he never considered retiring.

Some days, he seemed like he was doing great, and sometimes he was clearly struggling. If you know anybody who has had Parkinson's, you probably know: Sometimes it's unthinkably awful, but there are times during the day, when the person is rested and all the medicines and stars are aligned, he can function pretty well. For my dad, that was the afternoon. He would take a nap before he went to the ballpark. You had to tiptoe around the couch so you didn't wake him.

He couldn't get enough of being around the batting cage or introducing himself to new players. He just loved being around the scene. He would get his insulin shot from the Cardinals trainer Barry Weinberg, eat peanut butter in the clubhouse, and talk to George Kissell. George was just about the only person who worked for the Cardinals longer than my dad did, in almost every capacity, from minor-league manager to minor-league instructor. He was a legend in St. Louis.

My dad would joke about his physical condition. He would say, "At night, I don't say good night to my wife—I say good-bye." He would climb into bed with my mom and do play-by-play of his different medicines and ailments playing baseball against one another:

"Sinemet is on the mound . . . Pacemaker is on first . . . insulin's on third. Here comes Sinemet with the pitch . . ."

He worked well into his seventies, and it became pretty clear he would work until he couldn't work anymore. He always felt he had something to give. He proved it in one of our country's darkest hours.

———————

On September 11, 2001, I dropped Natalie off at school. She had just turned five. I found out on the radio about the Twin Towers being hit. When the first plane hit, I thought it was an accident—at that time, no one's minds automatically jumped to terrorism. I thought, "Oh, my God. Some plane got terribly off course and slammed into the World Trade Center." I went home and started watching this tragedy unfold on TV, and when the second plane hit, I, like everyone, knew it had to be terrorism.

I remember driving down to Busch Stadium when baseball resumed after the six-day layoff, thinking, "I have a wife and two kids, and I'm going into this public place with fifty thousand people. We're sitting ducks. Anything could happen." I felt myself getting obsessed about what might happen next. I was nervous driving down there. It felt like the end of the world was imminent.

I was going to do the game on TV, and my dad would do it on radio. But first, there was a pregame ceremony.

My father wrote a lot of poems late in his life. Some were really clever. Some were kind of silly. Some were dramatic. The poems were pretty simple—it wasn't like he had mastered iambic pentameter—but he enjoyed writing them.

So when 9/11 happened, he wrote a poem about it. I wasn't surprised. He was intensely patriotic, and 9/11 hit him on a really profound level. He must have read his poem to somebody with the Cardinals, because they asked him to read it before the game.

He was an emotional person on his calmest day. We used to joke that he would cry at the sight of a good kick return. To hear his own voice echoing through this stadium, reading a poem about terrorism and about what was just done to the United States, while his hands were shaking because of Parkinson's . . . I didn't think he would get through it.

I went out of my way to find him before he went down there, to say, "Are you sure you want to do this?"

He said, "I want to do this."

I said, "You're going to cry."

He put his paper down, and he put his finger one millimeter from my nose and gave me this dead-serious look, with his eyes narrowed, and he said, "I will not cry." His teeth were clenched.

I said, "You're going to cry."

And he said, "I will not cry. I'll bet you a hundred dollars."

I said, "OK. I'll bet you a hundred dollars."

He went down there and read it:

> Since this nation was founded under God
> More than two hundred years ago
> We have been the bastion of freedom
> The light that keeps the free world aglow
>
> We do not covet the possessions of others
> We are blessed with the bounty we share
> We have rushed to help other nations
> Anything, anytime, anywhere

War is just not our nature
We won't start, but we will end the fight
If we are involved
We shall be resolved
To protect what we know is right

We have been challenged by a cowardly foe
Who strikes and then hides from our view
With one voice we say
We have no choice today
There is only one thing to do

Everyone is saying
The same thing and praying
That we end these senseless moments we are living
As our fathers did before
We shall win this unwanted war
And our children will enjoy the future we'll be giving

He didn't cry.

But I did.

He came back up and stuck his hand out, like: "Where's my hundred?"

I just slapped him on the hand. I didn't have a hundred dollars on me.

That poem meant a lot to people, especially in St. Louis—but really, to baseball fans all over. The 9/11 attacks felt like a tragedy on two fronts. First and foremost was the incomprehensible murder of three thousand innocent people. But there was also the sense that the American way of life was under attack, and that we were doomed to live in fear. Our faith in one another, and in our country, was being tested. The poem kind of gave the signal that it was OK to enjoy baseball, or any kind of entertainment, again.

And he had the stature and authority to make the point. My father was, in many ways, the embodiment of the American dream. He grew up poor in the Depression, worked his way through college, and served our country in World War II. He was shot during his service, but he recovered and built a career, mostly in our national pastime.

As corny as it may sound, everything in his life kind of led to that moment, and he funneled it into that poem. People remember Mike Piazza's home run for the Mets in the first game in New York after those attacks, and they remember my dad's poem. In some small way, they both made America feel whole again.

Baseball was on the way to one of its strangest and most memorable finishes to a season. It was certainly so for me. But the first postseason moment I remember from that year was beyond strange. It was horribly embarrassing.

In Game 5 of the 2001 National League Division Series, Arizona's Tony Womack hit a series-winning single against St. Louis. As he celebrated on the field, a woman joined him and he hugged her.

And then I asked him if the woman, who was actually his wife, was his mom.

Uh . . . did I say mom? I . . . uh . . . meant . . . uh . . .

I was mortified. That was about as big, bad, awkward, and stupid as a live TV interview can be. You have to be a *moron* to say that. It was like accidentally walking into the women's restroom on national television. Or asking a woman when the baby is due, and having her say she isn't pregnant.

I said something like "Oh, my God. I'm sorry. Well, she's a fine-looking lady!"

How often do you see a broadcaster put his size 11 shoe in his mouth like that?

This was 100 percent my fault.

But I can explain. Sort of.

Tony's dad had died that year, around Father's Day. It really hit Tony hard. We were telling the story on the air right before he got the series-winning hit. He came around to home plate. At FOX, we love to take the viewers where they can't otherwise go, as quickly as possible, so as soon as the game ended, we threw a headset on him.

I was still up in the booth. I was thinking about his parents, his father dying, and the emotion of the moment. He was sobbing into the arms of this woman. I was interviewing him from the booth, and thus looking at them from up high. In the celebration, they all seemed like kids to me. Subconsciously, I was thinking, "Well, I'm sure he's not married, he's just a kid having fun playing Major League Baseball."

So I said on the air, "Hey, Tony, how does that feel?"

He said, "Oh, man, that's the biggest hit of my life. Unbelievable, ending a playoff series like that."

"Who are you hugging down there? Is that your mom?"

I could sense very quickly that I had done something wrong. When Tony said, "No, man, that's my wife," I went into full-on "Oh shit!" mode.

I was lucky that social media did not exist. People talked about it a bit, but the mechanism wasn't there to completely destroy me.

After the game, I went running down to the clubhouse, an odd combination of red-faced and white-faced, to apologize to Tony in person. Players were drinking champagne and celebrating. It was one of the great moments of their careers, and one of the worst of mine.

I pulled Tony over to the side. I said, "Look, I hope you know that I was thinking about your dad. Please tell your wife I'm so sorry. I'm so embarrassed. That's the most embarrassing thing I've ever done on TV."[26]

Under very rare circumstances, a man has a right to punch another man in the face. I would have understood if Tony had come at me with a left hook.

Instead, he said, "Oh, she's fine. Don't worry about it."

He was unbelievable. I ended up sending her flowers with an apology. Three years later, he got traded to the Cardinals. We got to know each other relatively well. He couldn't be a better guy.

The Diamondbacks made it all the way to the World Series to play the Yankees, who were going for their fourth straight World Series title. Normally, almost everybody in the country would be rooting against the Yankees. It's an American tradition. But in the wake of 9/11, it was hard for anybody to root against New York.

---

26. I didn't feel the need to explain that the bass-fishing contest might still be number one.

After the first two games in Arizona, both of which the Diamondbacks won, I flew to New York for Game 3. It was a strange feeling, being in the middle of this enormous entertainment vehicle while everybody is worried about 9/11, anthrax attacks, and a potential war in the Middle East.

I happened to be on the same flight as actor Jason Patric.[27] I've been a big fan of his for a long time, going back to *The Lost Boys*. I've watched some of his movies over and over, and there he was. But I didn't know him, and I sure wasn't going to say, "Hey, you're Jason Patric, on the same flight as me! Let's get drunk!"

Then, at the end of the flight, he came up to me. He said he was a Yankee fan and enjoyed our FOX broadcasts. And I thought: "Hey, you're Jason Patric, on the same flight as me! Let's get drunk!"

And so we did. We shared a ride into the city. I dropped my bags off at my hotel, and we went out and started running around the city. I think it started because we were kind of nervous, being in New York so soon after 9/11. We joked that we had to keep drinking until another terrible thing happened. It doesn't sound funny now, but I was about to broadcast World Series games at Yankee Stadium, everybody was worried about terrorists and bombs, and the whole country was just on edge. We needed to ease the tension a bit.

I had never seen security like they had at Yankee Stadium for Game 3. I had Cipro in my bag, because that was the antibiotic of choice in case there was an anthrax attack. We were all worried about it. It was a crazy time.

When I arrived at the ballpark, I didn't know that President

---

27. Name-dropping alert!

George W. Bush was coming to throw the first pitch. Then his helicopter landed out in left field, and he walked out of the Yankees dugout with his FDNY jacket on.

Throwing out the first pitch is hard, partly because it seems easy. From the stands, it looks like a simple throw, but doing something like that in front of a full stadium is nerve-racking. I was a pretty good high school pitcher, but when I threw the first pitch out at Busch Stadium, I almost passed out because I was so nervous. Stadiums mess with your depth perception, too. Even good athletes bounce it or throw it over the head of the catcher.

And this was an especially nervous moment, because it seemed very possible that Al Qaeda would attack Yankee Stadium during the World Series, or that somebody would spread anthrax around.

Most people stand between home plate and the mound and throw a first pitch. But President Bush, who played high school baseball, confidently walked straight to the mound, stood on the rubber, and gave the crowd a thumbs-up. Then he calmly fired a real sixty-foot, six-inch strike. It was stunning. We later heard that Derek Jeter told him something like "You can't bounce it. They'll boo you. You can't be in front of the mound. They'll boo you for that, too." But we didn't know that at the time. We just knew the president had thrown a strike, and that was one of the most powerful moments I've ever witnessed in sports. It was spine-tingling, and it had nothing to do with politics.

That night, Patric and I got drunk again after the game. The next night, Jeter won Game 4 in the tenth inning with that little home run into right, just after the clock struck midnight on Halloween—that's what earned him the nickname Mr. November. It was one of the most exciting games I've ever called, and to celebrate, Patric and I got drunk again.

I didn't even sleep long enough to wake up with bad breath. I was dragging ass to the stadium just to get there. Then the Yankees' Scott Brosius won Game 5 with a home run in the twelfth, and guess what. Patric and I got drunk again. I don't think I slept eight hours, total, in those three nights. The world was so tense, and I was so nervous going to New York, but once I got there, I felt kind of free and clear in the city. There weren't a lot of people out. We were running around the town having fun. I've never gone on a bender like that since. It's not sustainable. For whatever reason, I did it that week.

We caught a big broadcasting break that year with the World Series matchup. Obviously, the Yankees making the World Series so soon after 9/11 was compelling television. But the other break was that their opponent, the Diamondbacks, were managed by Bob Brenly.

Bob had worked on our number two announcing team with Thom Brennaman, and he had joined Tim and me in the booth for some playoff games. Brenly was a fantastic friend, and he understood and respected what we were trying to do.

We said: "Hey, Bob, remember us? Why don't you wear a microphone during the game?" He agreed to do it, as long as we didn't air anything live. That way, he could be himself. If he said something that didn't belong on the air or could get him in trouble, he trusted us enough to know we wouldn't air it.

The deal appeared to pay off in Game 4. Curt Schilling was pitching on short rest in New York. Nobody knew how long he would last, or how well he would pitch. Even the best starters often struggle on short rest.

Schilling was fantastic. Through seven innings, he had allowed only one run and thrown only 88 pitches. But Brenly replaced him with Byung-Hyun Kim.

"This is a decision that I do not agree with," I said on the air.

We then showed their exchange from a few minutes earlier. Brenly had walked up to Schilling in the dugout to tell him he was making a change, and Schilling objected. Brenly's microphone caught the whole conversation.

"That's enough, that's enough," Brenly said.

"No! No!" Schilling said. "I'm all right! I'm all right!"

Brenly said, "Listen, you're at eighty-eight [pitches] right now. We've got BK locked and loaded for the last six outs."

It was great theater. It belonged on Broadway. And like a lot of what you see on Broadway, it was fictional.

Here is what we didn't know. Earlier in that inning, Schilling had told his catcher, Damian Miller, that he was running out of gas: "Whatever happens, this is my last inning. Don't let him put me back out there again." Naturally, Miller had told Brenly.

Schilling wanted no part of that eighth inning. He was wiped out. And he knew Brenly wouldn't put him back out there, because he had told Miller not to let that happen.

But Schilling could see the microphone on Brenly's uniform. He knew he would look better if he begged to keep pitching on national television. So he asked Brenly to keep him in the game, and it was all bullshit. They both knew he was coming out.

Kim gave up the lead in the ninth inning, and Derek Jeter won the game with a home run off Kim in the tenth. Brenly got lots of heat for pulling Schilling against his will—the whole country had heard Schilling protest in the dugout. But Brenly couldn't really call out one of his aces for being a glory hound. He had to take the heat, and he did—with a great sense of humor.

"You fucking guys," he said with a laugh the next time we saw him. "You make me look like the bad guy. Never again!" He thought it was hilarious.

This wild, exhausting, depressing, terrifying, inspiring, thrilling, alcohol-soaked postseason ended in dramatic fashion, with the single greatest moment a television analyst has ever had.

That's my opinion anyway. I've never seen anything like what Tim McCarver did at the end of Game 7 of the 2001 World Series.

The Yankees led the Diamondbacks, 2–1, in the bottom of the ninth inning. Mariano Rivera was pitching for the Yankees. Somehow, the Diamondbacks tied the game and loaded the bases for their best hitter, Luis Gonzalez. There was one out.

Joe Torre, the Yankees manager, brought the infield in, so his infielders could make a throw to the plate and keep their season alive.

After Rivera's first pitch to Gonzalez, Tim said, "The one problem is, Rivera throws inside to left-handers. Left-handers get a lot of broken-bat hits in the shallow outfield . . . that's the danger of bringing the infield in with a guy like Rivera on the mound."

On the next pitch—the next pitch!—Gonzalez hit a broken-bat single just over Derek Jeter's head.

Viewers heard me say, "Floater . . . center field! The Diamondbacks are world champions!" They did not see me give Tim a high five. What an amazing moment for him. It was probably the highlight of my whole time with Tim. It was also the last World Series play that my father ever saw.

I remember when my maternal grandfather died. I was fifteen. I watched my dad get ready for the funeral, combing his hair very deliberately. I was always fascinated by which strand he would pick to go westward and start the part.

He saw that I was watching him.

"I know what you're thinking," he said. "You're thinking about what it's going to be like when *I* die."

That was *exactly* what I was thinking.

"When I die, you'll be ready for it," he said. "You'll handle it."

Part 4

Good-bye, Dad

Chapter 10

The Last Fight

Ann and I were down in the Florida Keys when we missed the call from my dad. I called him back and heard the voice of a younger Jack Buck. I had not heard his voice that strong in ten years.

He said, "Well, Buck, I went to the doctor today, and I want to let you know that I got diagnosed with lung cancer. It's contained in the bottom part of my lung, in one of the lobes of my lung. We're going to fight it. Everything will be well."

My dad, who cried so easily that we used to tease him about it, wasn't weepy about having cancer. He said, "We're going to be fine. I'm going to battle it and we'll get it taken out and we'll move on. Enjoy your vacation."

I hung up the phone.

Ann said, "What was that about?"

I said, "Well, my dad just told me he's got lung cancer."

He was seventy-seven, and he'd been struggling with Parkinson's disease and diabetes. When he called a game, he used every ounce of energy he had that day. But it kept him young. The clubhouse speakers would play Nelly, Run-D.M.C., Eminem—all these different rappers that he tolerated through the years. He loved being around the players. He loved introducing himself to new players on both teams.

And when he was out, nothing slowed him down. He wanted to sign every autograph and do every interview. His hand would shake, but he wasn't self-conscious. He told me that when you have Parkinson's, at some point you have to decide, "Screw it, I'm going to do what I do. Let them worry about the shaking." He would joke about it, too. It all disguised the reality, which is that he was nearing the end of his life.

In the Keys, I thought about his words to me when I was fifteen: *When I die, you'll be ready for it. You'll handle it.* I hoped he was right. I would do my best. But I would also have to deal with all the people who thought he was family—and a few who thought he wasn't family *enough*.

Shortly after the diagnosis, I was in a waiting room at Barnes-Jewish Hospital with most of my half brothers and half sisters. A doctor came out and said an issue had come up during surgery.

"We're going back in," he said.

My mom was crying. I was nervous. And that's when I heard my half siblings muttering, loud enough for my mom to hear it: "*I knew this was wrong.*" . . . "*We shouldn't have done it this way.*" . . . "*This is the wrong doctor. . . .*"

I stood up, and for the first time, thirty-two years of tension bubbled over. I was so mad they were questioning my mom.

"How dare you?" I said. "How dare you after all these years?! You missed birthdays! You missed everything! And you sit here and armchair-quarterback the only person who has always done everything she can to protect our father!"

It got heated. I mean, I just *lost* it. I was yelling at them in that waiting room: "You've never been there for anything! Now we're here because he's sick and you want to judge everything! We have the best doctors this city has to offer!"

I ended up taking it outside the room to the cafeteria, to talk it over with my half sister Christine's husband, David. I calmed down after that.

What could I do? I do have empathy for my half siblings, because they didn't get to know my dad the way I got to know him. I'm not sure *anybody* in my family got to know him the way I got to know him. But when they were kids, he was new to town, finding his way, working constantly. His career didn't really take off until around the time he met my mom.

My sister got to know him well, but I think I knew him even better, because I got to go on more road trips with him when I was a kid, and then even more when we were broadcast partners.

My father came from nothing, worked like crazy, and had a taste of success. He had fun. Even when he met my mom, he maintained that kind of Johnny Carson swashbuckling demeanor, where every night felt like an adventure. My half siblings missed that.

Even though he wasn't home with Julie and me a lot, I'm sure he stayed home more with us than he did when he lived with his older kids. I just don't think my half siblings ever knew what they had in their dad. I don't think they ever got past the hurt of him meeting my mom. And I can't fault them for that. But I was astonished that all these years, even as he lay dying, some of them were still hanging on to that. I felt like, if they were still resentful when he was on his death-bed, then that was it—they would *always* be resentful.

But as my dad had told my mom, so many years ago: *So what?* I tried to treasure my own relationship with him as long as I could, and so much of it was built around laughter. I remember him being wheeled out of surgery, and I said, "Dad, are you feeling all right? Your color's great."

He said, "Really? What color am I?"

I joked, "A nice shade of green."

He laughed and said, "Just wheel me right out the fucking window."

I was lucky that I could connect with him like that, all the way to the end. But I knew I would still have to share him with the city. I knew that when he died, it would be different from when somebody else's dad died. All of St. Louis would want to pull up a chair and mourn with us.

"Will your dad be ready for Opening Day?"

It was early 2002. Dan Caesar of the *Post-Dispatch* was on the phone. Old wounds do heal eventually; I came to see Dan's point in his original critique of me, and I came to like him personally. And now he wanted to know when my father would be back in the Cardinals broadcast booth.

I tried to be honest: "Look, I don't want you writing this . . . this is off the record . . ."

I didn't want to sound the alarms. I tried to be as vague as I could but still give him some kind of update, both as a courtesy to Dan and because everybody wanted to know.

My dad had been doing Cardinals games for almost fifty years. He was a part of people's lives. I think St. Louis is the smallest big town in the country. Everybody knows everything about everyone. You go to the grocery store, and people know what kind of fruit you like.

I was never totally comfortable with that kind of attention, but my dad enjoyed it. I think the adulation kept him going. It gave him strength. I hope that doesn't sound strange. But when your body is breaking down, and you know you are near the end of your life, it's good to have daily reminders that your existence is meaningful to other people.

He wanted to do good, and raise money for causes he believed in, and he never wanted to stop. St. Louis is a really philanthropic town, and my dad became the unofficial charity emcee for the whole city. There was a time, early in his career, when he was doing three or four banquets a week. He hosted a golf tournament to benefit a cystic-fibrosis charity for more than twenty years. Whatever the cause, he was there.

The night before he went in for his first lung cancer surgery, he did a banquet at the Missouri Athletic Club, one of those old-time clubs that goes back to the early twentieth century. The banquet was named after him. The club has a restaurant that is also named after him. They gave out the Sports Personality of the Year Award at the banquet, and they would honor one top athlete every year, and it was up to my dad to make sure the athlete showed up. So in 2001, he emceed it, left the banquet, and drove straight to Barnes-Jewish Hospital to check in for surgery.

He did not tell anybody at the dinner he had lung cancer. Even when he was in the hospital, dying, he was raising money for the Mathews-Dickey Boys' & Girls' Club.

So people in St. Louis had a lot of reasons to wonder if my dad was OK. That's why Dan Caesar wanted to know if Dad would be ready for Opening Day.

I was thinking, "Opening Day? I just hope he makes it out of the hospital." But I couldn't say that. It would have created a stir we didn't need.

My dad got discharged from the hospital after the surgery, but he got an infection a few days later and went back in. He would be in that hospital for the rest of his life. We got him outside one time, because it was a beautiful day and because he was Jack Buck and the hospital staff wanted to do that for him. But it took three people, with the machines and a ventilator. I will never forget the look on his face as he finally breathed in the fresh air on a perfect day in St. Louis. He kept mouthing the word *wow*, and tears filled his eyes.

He lived for seven months after the initial diagnosis. I wish he hadn't. He was so unhappy. He had Sundowning syndrome and didn't know if it was day or night or what month it was.

He would tell me that his friend Bob Goalby, the golfer, was on his ceiling.

I tried to reason with him: "Dad . . ."

He was mouthing everything because of his tracheotomy tube: "I'm telling you, before you leave here you'll see him."

I said, "*DAD.*"

After a few weeks in the hospital, his hair was getting kind of shaggy. So I brought in a friend, Julie, who cut my hair. She was one of the few people who got to see him in the hospital. He was so sick and so tired, and his legs weren't working. He couldn't even sit up long enough to get through a haircut. We had to bail on the idea.

What happened next still amazes me: He underwent a brain operation, where he had to sit there for six or seven hours to get these electrodes in his head to calm the Parkinson's symptoms. They were trying to stop the tremors, with the hope that would help him get off the ventilator. He was awake. They would zap the electrode, or whatever the hell it was, and ask him: "Can you feel this in your foot? . . . Raise your right hand." And he would respond.

I can't believe he did it. What incredible resolve. But it also changed his personality. He seemed like a different person. He barely blinked after that.

We didn't allow many visitors, but there were a few exceptions. Stan Musial, St. Louis's best and most-loved athlete, brought a bag of baseballs that he signed, and handed them to the entire staff. He said, "Just make sure you take care of this man." Stan was the sweetest guy of all time. My father would perk up when he came by.

We tried everything to get him healthy. At one point they took out his pacemaker to get an infection down so they could do the brain operation. Think of how harrowing that sentence is.

I discovered the excruciating difference between being alive and being able to live. They kept my dad alive. But he was not really able to live.

At one point, Steve Miller, who was then head of Barnes-Jewish Hospital, came to me. I'd met him through Steve Horn (who had family members treated at Barnes), and he was such a nice man.

Miller said, "We are dedicated to giving him the best care that we can give him. And we will continue to do so as long as you want to. But I'm going to tell you, as your friend, despite whatever any other doctor's telling you: He will never get out of here. I'm not forcing your hand, but you may want to start to think about how to gracefully end this."

That was sobering. A week later, I stopped in the hospital after a Cardinals game. I liked to go in then, late at night, because it was quiet.

My father mouthed: "Will you do me a favor?"

I said, "Absolutely. Whatever you need."

He mouthed again: "Will you *promise* me you'll do me a favor?"

I said, "Yes, whatever you want."

Then he paused and mouthed:

"Will . . . you . . . let . . . me . . . die?"

What do you say to that? I acted like I didn't understand what he was asking me. I said, "What?" But I knew what he had said. I just wanted to see if he would say it again.

He mouthed it again: "Will you let me die?"

And I said, "Dad, we've got the best doctors; I know it's frustrating . . ."

He waved his hands like: *I don't want to hear that.* My dad, one of the most upbeat people I've ever met, said, "Just let me die."

I said, "Here's the deal I'll make you. If in two weeks, this isn't better, then we'll revisit this." It was a stall tactic.

He brushed me off, and we talked for a few minutes—about my life, the Cardinals, whatever. I don't remember.

Shortly after that, he started having a series of strokes. That altered his personality, too. At the end of his life, he became almost like a child. I'm sure that made him vulnerable.

I didn't tell anybody he had asked me to let him die. I kept that to myself. But two weeks later, my mom was in his hospital room with him, and he got angry with her.

"I know what you and Joe are trying to do to me," he mouthed to her. "I've been told by people, and I know *exactly* what you're trying to do."

My mom said, "What are you talking about?"

And my father said, "I know you and Joe are trying to kill me."

My mom called me, crying. I said he was on so many medications and had suffered so many strokes, he didn't even know what he was saying.

I said, "Mom, he's not right. This isn't him."

Then I told her: "Two weeks ago he was begging me to let him die. This is a different person we're talking to."

My mom told him, "Oh, Jack. All I want is for you to come home."

But it had become clear that he would never come home. My father—

a man who was wounded in the Battle of Remagen, which helped end World War II, a man who had earned a Purple Heart—was not much more than a skeleton. He must have weighed less than ninety pounds.

We had to pick a day to end his life. We settled on June 18, 2002.

On the evening of June 17, I visited my dad with my wife and my sister. I knew the next day would be the last day of his life. Julie and Ann left, and I sat there and talked with my father—more *to* him than *with* him, really, because he was basically out of it. I told him how much I loved him, how much I appreciated all that he'd given me, and that I wouldn't be where I was without all those hours he had spent with me.

I told him he was my best friend.

I walked out and decided that would be it—the last time I would see my dad. I didn't want to go back the next day. I didn't want to be around my half brothers and half sisters to see who cried the loudest. There was no need for me to see him take his last breath. This wasn't a movie. I had said what I needed to say.

At 9:00 A.M. the next day, they pulled out all the tubes. All my half brothers and half sisters were there, along with Julie and my mom. I was just waiting for updates on my phone, for the news that would hit me before it shook St. Louis: Jack Buck was gone.

An hour passed. Two hours. It was early afternoon, and he was still alive. Soon it was 3:00 P.M. . . . 4:00 P.M. . . . 5:00 P.M. . . . 6:00 P.M. No word.

The Cardinals had a home game at 7:00 P.M., against the Angels, and I was scheduled to do the TV broadcast. I knew he would not want me to miss a day of work. I went on the air.

As the game got under way, the nurses pulled a TV down by his head with the Cardinals game on.

My dad's heart kept beating. He was not responsive, and he was not making eye contact . . . but he was breathing on his own. He had not done that in six months. On the TV by his head, I was broadcasting this matchup between the Cardinals' Darryl Kile and the Angels' Kevin Appier like it was any other casual summer night.

During a break in the fourth or fifth inning, I told my partner in the booth, Al Hrabosky: "My dad's going to die tonight. I can't believe he hasn't passed away already."

Al broke down and cried.

I didn't. I kept doing the Cardinals game.

The game ended. Still no word from the hospital. I got in my car, and . . . *Dammit.* Barnes-Jewish was exactly midway between my house and Busch Stadium. It's right on Highway 40. It was looming there, daring me to drive past it rather than visit my dad one last time.

I said, "Screw it. I'm going to go again." My mom and sister had told me the rest of my family had left the hospital. It would just be me and him.

I pulled in, parked illegally, and went up to his room. For the first time in months, there were no tubes and no beeping. He was just tucked in under this white blanket and white sheet. There was a monitor showing his blood oxygen, the only real confirmation that he was alive.

I walked in. The nurses got up and left. They, too, were stunned he was still alive. I bent down and whispered in his ear:

"Dad, it's time to go. This has been an unbelievable fight. You continue to show your strength every time the sun comes up. You've done it again. I'm here to tell you it's time to go. And it's OK.

"I've got everybody covered. Mom's fine. We all love you, but it's time to go. If you're worried about anything, don't be. I'll handle it.

"I love you. Thanks for being my best friend."

I kissed him on the forehead, stood up, and walked out. By the time I got into my car, he had died.

My dad was gone, but the public character of "Jack Buck" still had to die. On my way home, I called KMOX, the radio station that had carried Cardinals games forever. That's what my dad would have wanted. I told the overnight host, John Carney, my father had died.

He said, "Will you come on?"

I said, "Yeah, I will."

So when I got home a few minutes later, I sat on the floor in my bedroom, in the dark, and let Carney interview me about my dad's death. It was a good interview—John handled it really well. But for me, it was so weird. When I was three years old, my dad told me I could sit on the floor in his office while he did a radio interview, as long as I kept quiet. Now I was sitting on the floor at age thirty-two, doing a radio interview about him dying.

It was like I went from being this man's son to being his broadcast partner and then to a reporter covering his death.

Logically, I should have been crying. I'm usually an easy cry, like my dad was. When somebody wins on *American Idol*, my tear ducts open up. It must be hereditary. But I wasn't crying. I was talking on the radio with a steady, calm, professional voice.

I didn't cry at all when my dad died. Not once. I think it was because I had months to prepare, but also because I was like that three-year-old again, or like the teenage kid who was scared to get in trouble because it would reflect poorly on his father. He had raised me to be professional and composed, and I couldn't really shut that off and just be devastated.

Normally when a loved one dies, friends and acquaintances help you get through it. This was the opposite. I had to help them. His wake was at Busch Stadium. I emceed it. All my half brothers and sisters were there, and of course my mom, Mike Shannon, Dan Dierdorf, Bob Costas . . . all these people who knew him well, and thousands of others who *thought* they knew him well. The Cardinals were there, and somebody took a picture of them leaning over a railing, watching the wake. The most prominent player in the photo is Darryl Kile, who was pitching the night my dad died.

In the funeral procession going out to Jefferson Barracks, I realized how many people my dad had touched. There were people who stopped off on the side of the highway, people waving flags. It was mind-blowing.

How many of them interrupted our dinner at Cunetto's once, and carried that memory with them forever? How many saw him in an airport or on the street and told him a story? How many were stunned when they ran into him again, years later, and he remembered their name and their story? How many just listened to KMOX every night in the summer and felt like he was part of their family?

I got bags of mail. I didn't get through it all until a couple of months after he died. I got handwritten letters from Bill Clinton and Billy Crystal. Clinton wrote about growing up as a Cardinals fan in Arkansas, listening to my dad and Harry Caray. When you do a game, you don't think about some future president listening on his radio. But that's what happened.

I sat in my office and went through one letter after another, people pouring their hearts out about what he meant to them.

Whether it's Vin Scully in Los Angeles or Ernie Harwell in Detroit, local baseball announcers can have that kind of impact on people. This was especially true in the 1970s and 1980s, before there were a million TV channels and the Internet. But I think, even among that group, my dad was different. He was not just a voice. He interacted with his listeners all the time. If there was a cause, or there was a chance to raise money for something, and somebody asked him to do it, he'd do it. He didn't ask a ton of questions, and he rarely said no. And I think that generosity really touched people.

He was loved. And he loved being loved. I'm sure a therapist would have told him that, if he'd ever seen a therapist. And I *guarantee* he never saw a therapist.

The day after the wake, I went to a sub shop with my wife and kids, and after I waited in line for our sandwiches, my daughter, Natalie, said she wanted chips, too. I didn't see the point in waiting in the sandwich line again just to order chips. I grabbed a bag of chips and went up to the cash register, and this customer in line started barking at me:

"Hey, we're all waiting in line here. You think you're better than everybody else?"

I said, "I've already waited in this line. I'm getting chips for my daughter. We've already—"

"Get in the back of the line!"

"I'm just getting chips—"

"You just fucking think you're better than everybody!"

I was frazzled and drained. I said, "This has been a long week, man."

He said, "I don't give a shit about your week!"

I bought the chips. He kept going: "I'm going to kick your ass!"

He was threatening to kick my ass over chips! It was crazy.

I said, "I just had somebody die in my family."

He said, "I don't give a *fuck* about your family."

It's amazing what you remember. I felt there was one guy in the whole city who didn't know my dad died, and he was threatening to kill me. It stuck with me.

The next day was the funeral. My half sister Christine gave this beautiful eulogy. I spoke after her, and I ad-libbed my first line, like my father would have: "It's a bad feeling sitting there in the front row, knowing that the eulogy I'm listening to is ten times better than the one I'm about to give. Christine was great. Here's what I've got." But I was proud of my eulogy.

People told me all these stories I never heard about my dad, just different things he'd done around the city, small acts of kindness that make a son proud. That weekend, I was supposed to broadcast the Cardinals game in Chicago. I flew up there. Gary Lang at FOX Sports put together this beautiful video tribute to my dad. It had pictures of him as a young man; in World War II; and with his family. It showed him reciting the poem he wrote after 9/11, and him skydiving on his seventy-fifth birthday, with his own voice as the voice-over: "You go, and go, and go, and pretty soon you're gone . . . Adios, Momma." That was the closest I came to crying.

I was getting ready to do the game when we found out it was canceled.

Darryl Kile had died. He had a heart attack in his hotel room.

My father lived to be seventy-eight. He had a fantastic life. Darryl was thirty-three, just a few months older than I was. He left behind a wife and three young kids. *That* was a real tragedy. My dad's story was just life. I was reminded, again, how lucky I've been.

Part 5

The Top

Chapter 11

This Thing Is Huge

While my dad was in the hospital, Pat Summerall did his final game for FOX—the Super Bowl between the Rams and the Patriots. My bosses, David Hill and Ed Goren, made it clear they wanted me to replace Summerall and work with John Madden, who was the best ever in an NFL booth, on the number one team. It was an elevated role, and it meant I would do the Super Bowl every third year.

I was excited to work with Madden. But we never did a game together. Shortly after Summerall retired, Madden left for ABC and *Monday Night Football.*

I don't think Madden had any personal or professional problem with me, but I do think he was wary of our partnership, and here is why: He had worked with Summerall for two decades. He had one partner that entire time. And with my baseball postseason commitment, I had to walk away from the NFL for a month every season. I don't think Madden wanted to work with one play-by-play guy most of the season and somebody else in October.

When Madden left, FOX thought about replacing him with Bill Parcells. In his hospital bed, my dad loved the idea. Parcells was one of his favorite coaches. They got along really well. Parcells would tell him things about the inner workings of his team's locker room—who was playing well, who wasn't, how he dealt with Lawrence Taylor, that kind of thing. Parcells trusted my father. My dad was so excited we might work together, but that fell through, too.

Instead, FOX put me in a booth with Troy Aikman and Cris Collinsworth. I would not have asked for a three-man booth. No play-by-play announcer ever asks for that. I've done it in baseball, too, most recently with Harold Reynolds and Tom Verducci. We did our best, but a three-man booth is awkward. How do you have a normal conversation when you don't know who will speak next? The play-by-play announcer has to play traffic cop.

I learned that Troy and Cris were an interesting combination. Troy is so meticulous—he studies film and sees the game from a quarterback's perspective, and he can identify a defense's coverage in an instant. Every week, I could see why he won three Super Bowls and made the Hall of Fame.

And Cris was just the best pure broadcaster I've ever worked with. He is one of a handful of former players who could do play-by-play if you asked.[28] I really think Cris could do anything in broadcasting.

---

28. Summerall, Frank Gifford, and Dan Dierdorf are on that short list.

But Cris is also out for Cris, and I mean that in the best possible way. He is not selfish. But when he sees opportunity within a broadcast to make a statement that will be memorable, he makes it.

Troy doesn't need that. Troy made his name as a player, as a Super Bowl champion. Cris was a terrific player, but he wasn't Troy Aikman. I think Troy will always be remembered as a player, and Cris will be remembered as a broadcaster.

Troy doesn't want people talking about him after the broadcast. Early on, he made a comment during a *preseason* game, about Donovan McNabb's passing being inaccurate. It carried so much weight that the Philadelphia media were asking Donovan McNabb after the game in the press conference: Do you know what Troy Aikman said about you?

They love when a famous Cowboy criticizes an Eagle. It wouldn't have been a big deal if I had said it. But I'm not Troy Aikman.

Imagine how the Philadelphia media would have reacted if they knew Troy could have left our booth to play for the Eagles. It's true: One year, while we were doing a game in San Diego, the Eagles' Donovan McNabb got hurt. And at halftime of our game, Troy got a phone call from Eagles coach Andy Reid, asking if he wanted to come back and play.

Can you imagine that? Troy Aikman, Dallas Cowboy Hall of Famer, leaving the broadcast booth at the start of a season to go play for the rival Eagles. That would have been wild. And Troy loves Andy Reid. But he said no. He had moved on.

I did games with Troy and Cris for three years. Then Cris went to NBC. Nobody knew this at the time, but I had a chance to join him there.

In the winter of 2004–2005, NBC's Dick Ebersol asked to meet with me. Ebersol has had an incredible career, from working on *Saturday Night Live* to reinventing how the Olympics are covered. And now he needed a voice for his latest property: *Sunday Night Football*.

Ann and I met Ebersol in the basement of a restaurant in Manhattan. Ebersol had just lost his son Teddy in a plane crash in Colorado. He started talking about the accident, and he was so open about it. He said he almost died himself but was pulled out by one of his sons. He talked about what it was like to lose Teddy. Ann and I were young parents, and I don't really like to fly anyway. I don't know how you rebound from losing a child. I guess you just do it. I was amazed by Ebersol's strength, and I still am.

Eventually, he started talking about the far less consequential topic of *Sunday Night Football*. It was clearly going to be the new *Monday Night Football*—the premier prime-time NFL game each week, and one of the highest-rated shows, period. Ebersol basically told me the play-by-play job was mine if I wanted it.

I was extremely flattered. The insecure part of me felt good—this was a nice counter to everybody who said I got where I was only because I was Jack Buck's kid. Dick Ebersol didn't care about that. There was too much on the line for him.

The timing wasn't right—my contract was still a couple of years from being expired, and they needed a guy quickly. And I don't think I would have left anyway. I was the top guy at FOX, and I knew Bob Costas would always be the top guy at NBC. Plus, I would have to give up baseball. And I just didn't want to leave FOX. It was home for me. So I said no, Ebersol hired Al Michaels, and it's worked out great for everybody.

———————

As my dad lay dying, Ann and I were living in that nice house, the one my father had proclaimed was "too big." I never thought it was too big. It was certainly big enough, though. It was all we needed, despite my occasional golf course fantasies.

But we had money to burn, and financing my golf course fantasies could help us burn it. We found a piece of property right next to Old Warson Country Club, just as I had imagined. And we started building our dream house.

Dream house may be an understatement. You could have built a dream house *inside* our dream house. It was ridiculous and excessive. It didn't even feel quite right to me, even at the time.

I said to my father in the hospital, "Dad, this thing is huge."

He said, "I hope me laying here has taught you: When you're here, it's too late. Build your house. Live your life. Have your fun."

I took that as a sign of approval. And when we first looked at the plans, the house really didn't seem too big. Then we started building, and I thought, "Holy shit." It was more than 10,000 square feet, which is crazy. I started to sense that people were driving by and looking at it and saying, "Oh, that's Joe Buck's house." It was not a good feeling.

We moved in a few months after my dad died. We tried to make it feel like a home instead of a hotel, and I think for the most part we succeeded. It's not a formal house. It felt kind of like a lodge, which is what I always wanted. Give me a warm house with a great TV and a great couch, and deep down, that's what I really want.

We didn't do a lot of entertaining. My parents looked for any excuse to hire a piano player and throw a party, but Ann and I probably had two or three parties in a decade. That was it. My friends are scattered around the country, and I enjoy visiting all these different ports and seeing them. When I'm home, I just kind of want to be quiet. So it's not like I wanted to throw a bunch of parties in St. Louis for two hundred people.

And yet, there was no denying: The house was enormous. People talk about keeping up with the Joneses. I told Ann: "We *are* the Joneses." It felt like we were daring everybody in our friend group to keep up, and I wasn't interested in it. It's not how I grew up. It wasn't what I ever wanted. I didn't want the status of a big house. Maybe we did it because it felt like what we were supposed to do.

And of course, if you have an enormous house, you have to fill it. We kept getting deliveries of rugs and paintings and couches—it felt like we were constantly redecorating. I was fortunate to be making a lot of money, and we just kept spending it on what felt like a bunch of bullshit.

While we're on the topic of spending crazy amounts of money, let's talk about the Yankees and Red Sox. In the 2000s, the rivalry was both historic and fresh, and it was riveting. You couldn't script it and couldn't even imagine until it happened. They had been rivals forever, but this was different. The Yankees were the premier team in baseball again. The Red Sox were trying to catch them and win their first World Series since 1918.

Eventually, the rivalry would lose a bit of its appeal—you can't sustain that kind of tension forever, especially when (spoiler alert!) the Red Sox have ended their championship drought. But at the time, nobody knew if the Red Sox would ever win the World Series.

Those games were intense, and a joy to broadcast. And the fans were intense, too. Sometimes *too* intense. After one of the games in Boston in the middle of the 2003 American League Championship Series, I got out of a car across the street from our hotel, the XV Beacon. Two Boston fans were stumbling out of a bar. My eyes locked with one of them. He saw me and said:

"That's fucking Joe Buck."[29]

This guy started yelling at me: "You love the Yankees, you motherfucker! I'm going to kick your ass!"

Well, anybody can *say* that. But the two of them started walking toward me. Then they started jogging toward me. They were drunk and pissed off, which is never a good combination. I prefer drunk and happy. I had too much pride to run into the hotel like a terrified child, but I walked just fast enough to make it into the hotel right before they could pummel me for being a Yankees homer, which would have been ridiculous because everybody knows I'm a Cardinals homer.[30] Who has the energy to be a homer for two teams? That sounds exhausting.

The truth is, if I was rooting for anybody at that time, it was the Cubs. They were in the National League Championship Series against the Marlins. To me, the Cubs winning the World Series would be the greatest story in sports. I don't know what could beat that.

After Game 5 of Yankees–Red Sox in Boston, several of us from FOX were riding back from Boston to New York in a limousine. That's not our normal mode of transportation—that's the kind of thing you

---

29. My name is Joe Francis Buck, so technically, it's Joe F. Buck, not F. Joe Buck.
30. Some people in St. Louis say I hate the Cardinals. This is an unwinnable argument for me.

saw in the 1980s, when network spending accounts were at their peak. But it was cheaper than flying and easier than the train. There was a TV in the limo. The reception was crappy, but we watched the Cubs take a lead on the Marlins in Game 6. They had a chance to clinch a World Series bid, and they would either play the Red Sox in the all-time who-can-end-their-drought series, or they would play the Yankees in the all-time David versus Goliath series. I was fired up.

People were lined up on Waveland and Sheffield Avenues in Chicago, getting ready for history. Then there was this foul pop-up along the left-field line, and this Cubs fan named Steve Bartman reached out and grabbed it from the Cubs' Moises Alou, Alou got mad, and the whole team fell apart. I felt terrible for Bartman. And it seemed pretty clear, even before Game 6 ended, the Cubs would not win Game 7.

But we would still get the Yankees, the sport's premier team, or the Red Sox with a chance to end their World Series drought. The Yankees and Red Sox went back and forth in that series. There were so many great players and great characters: Pedro Martinez, Roger Clemens, Mariano Rivera, Derek Jeter, Manny Ramirez, David Ortiz.

Tim and I had a current player in the booth with us, as we often did during the postseason. It was Bret Boone. His brother, Aaron, happened to play for the Yankees, too, though nobody thought he was the main story, or even in the top ten.

Bret was fantastic company on the way to the stadium and on the way home. I always liked him. But he didn't want to be there as a broadcaster. He really didn't want to do any work for it. He was mailing it in, and I was getting annoyed.

The series went to a seventh game, which is the dream for any broadcasting team. A Game 7 between rivals really kind of broadcasts itself. But it's intense. We were getting ready in the booth before the game, and Bret was screwing around while we were trying to have a meeting.

I finally said, "Bret, come over here."

We went into the corner of the booth. I said, "Listen, unless you want me trying to turn a double play with you in Game 7 next year if you're in it, don't fuck around with this. This is our job. This is how we make our money. This is what we stake our reputation on, delivering a Game 7. If you want to fuck around, then *get out of here*. But if not, then either offer something that's helpful, give some insight, or sit there and shut the fuck up."

It was one of the few times I was a non-pleaser and confronted somebody. But I felt like I had to say it. I wasn't going to let him screw up Yankees–Red Sox Game 7.

Bret was taken aback. But during the course of the game, he was more serious. He stopped messing around. One thing Tim and I really prided ourselves on: The bigger the game, the less we talked. It was more dramatic that way.

Martinez was starting Game 7 for Boston. Clemens started for the Yankees. You can't beat that, and there is no point in hyping it. I told Tim and Bret, "I really don't even want to talk in the first inning when Pedro's pitching here in Yankee Stadium. Let's just let the crowd carry it."

We did that. I just wanted the crowd to be overwhelming in somebody's living room. And Bret got it. Finally.

The Red Sox took a 4–0 lead, but the Yankees came back and forced extra innings. Tim Wakefield was pitching to Aaron Boone,

Bret's little brother. Aaron hit a game-winning, series-winning, jinx-defining home run, and Yankee Stadium was *rocking*. Our booth was actually bouncing. It was insane.

As Aaron rounded the bases, we showed a shot of Bret in the booth. And we kept going back to him, hoping to capture the emotion of the moment. Imagine having Bobby Thomson's brother in the booth when he hit the "Shot Heard 'Round the World." It should have been great TV, but Bret was motionless. And Mike Weisman, our producer who is so funny, said, "Bret, you're on TV, smile or do some fucking thing." Bret barely moved. Maybe he wasn't sure what to do. But I also think that, because Bret is so competitive, part of him was thinking: "Why is that him and not me?"

The next year, the Yankees and Red Sox faced each other in the American League Championship Series again. This time, the Yankees won the first three games. Before Game 4, the Red Sox were joking about their fate by the batting cage. They were kidding around, saying, "Hey, watch out for us!"

Everybody assumed they were finished. And so did they.

Of course, they won four straight games to win the series, in one of the most dramatic comebacks ever. Since then, they have sold the story that they always knew they had a chance—that if they just won one game, they could win four. But that's complete crap. I watched them when they were down 3–0, and they looked beaten. They had just gotten crushed, 19–8, in Game 3. Some of the Red Sox wished the Yankees good luck in the World Series.

Downtown apartment living (just off my shift grabbing pennies out of onlookers' hands).

Age two? One of us is looking at the wrong camera.

Bad pants, tight shorts.

My parents with their adopted kids from Molasses Swamp (or fringe rhymes with singe—white-hot).

Mom, could you have found one salad bar in the late seventies?

Batboy shirt, Dave LaPoint's pants, multitasking—God forbid I take two trips to the dugout seven paces away.

Pregame catch at Busch Stadium with my friend Dave "Rooster" Rader—hot turf makes my bell-bottoms flare more.

Where it all began. Joe B and
Jim Kelch in the Louisville
broadcast booth, 1989.

My favorite picture. . . . My dad holding my
daughter Natalie, with me on TV during the
1996 postseason—and he acted like he didn't
watch—BUSTED!

© Colin Miller

Sorry . . . all I see is hair . . . is
my dad in the picture?

Emmy night. My dad and his Lifetime Emmy,
and me and my first Emmy. I don't know who
is more proud.

My original core four in a photo from the early 2000s.

Hi dad it's Trudy!
Your gonna do a
great job doing the
game today I just
Know it! I love you
So much and your
voice sounds so much
better that no one's
gonna tell that anythings
wrong ☺ with it!
Love
Trudy

The Canyon Suites at The Phoenician
6000 East Camelback Road Scottsdale, Arizona
p. 480.423.2880 f. 480.423.2881 canyonsuites.com

The girls at the 2005 World Series in
Chicago—Natalie is front runnin'.

A note that melted my heart.
Found in my scorebook be-
fore the 2011 MLB All-Star
Game in Phoenix, Arizona.

Natalie and me on Mount Kilimanjaro, February 2013.

Trudy and me in Amsterdam,
summer 2014.

My friend Artie and my daughter Natalie
at his interview show in New York City
(he is a bit more subdued than the first
time she saw him).

My new core four—without whom I am nothing—at the *NFL Honors* show before Super Bowl XLVIII in New York City.

My FOX football crew. Left to right: Ed Sfida (stats), Steve Horn (editorial notes), Dave Schwalbe (spotter), me, HOFer Troy Aikman, Scott Snyder (Troy's spotter), and Mike Pereira (rules genius). It takes a village.

Beach wedding at the El Dorado Golf and Beach Club in Cabo San Lucas with my beautiful best friend, April 2014.

See?!?! We are friends! JT, JB, and TMac before the 2011 MLB All-Star Game in Phoenix, Arizona.

My biggest fan, smartest critic, best support. The sweetest woman I know.

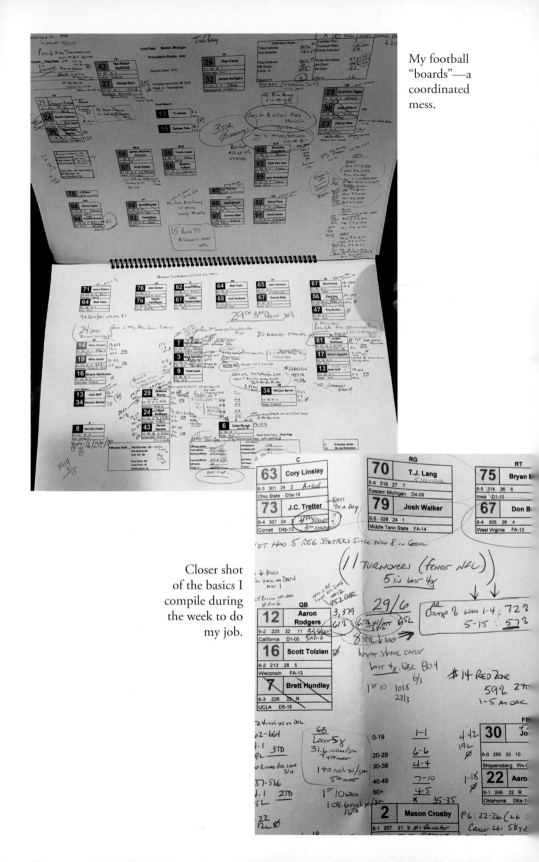

My football "boards"—a coordinated mess.

Closer shot of the basics I compile during the week to do my job.

But that is the beauty of baseball: Even the players don't know what they might pull off. The Red Sox were literally within a foot or so of being finished when Dave Roberts stole a base in the ninth inning of Game 4. They won that, won the next, and suddenly we had a series again.

I started to think the Red Sox would win it in Game 6. That was Curt Schilling's famous bloody-sock game—a tendon in Schilling's ankle needed repeated surgical stabilization in that postseason, and he started bleeding through his sock. I guess, when you think about Schilling's fake pleas to Bob Brenly's microphone three years earlier, he could have just put ketchup on his sock. I'm kidding. Schilling truly was remarkable to go through that and pitch as well as he did. What a competitor. And when the Red Sox won Game 6, I think we all expected them to win Game 7.

After the Red Sox won that Game 7, I flew home for Game 7 of the Cardinals-Astros National League Championship Series. The Cardinals' Scott Rolen hit a home run, and on the video board at Busch, they played a cut from a Budweiser commercial I had done before. In the commercial, my "agent" convinces me to use a catchphrase, and I come up with the utterly ridiculous "Slam-a-lama ding dong!" So on the video board at Busch, they showed me saying "Slam-a-lama," and then the whole crowd yelled, "Ding dong!"

It was really cool.

And I think that was the last time I was loved in St. Louis.

A few days later, the Red Sox swept the Cardinals for their first World Series title since 1918. I was the voice on TV capturing the moment—and to Cardinals fans, I was "celebrating" their team's loss.

In the eyes of a lot of Cardinals fans, I was betraying them and my family name. They don't understand: Rooting for the Cardinals or ANY team is not my job. I make the call to the best of my ability when it happens in front of me. I don't and can't care who wins. The fans do, however, and I'm glad they do.

Of all the teams that Tony La Russa managed in St. Louis, I thought that 2004 team was the best—way better than the 2006 and 2011 teams that won the World Series. It was just Boston's time.

For me personally, it was great to see Terry Francona win as manager of the Red Sox. I'd known him when he was a player—his dad played for the Cardinals—and I was broadcasting his games when I was nineteen and he played for the Louisville Redbirds. I thought he was as big a part of a World Series championship as any manager I have ever seen, because of the personalities he dealt with (Pedro Martinez, Curt Schilling, Manny Ramirez, David Ortiz) and the decisions he'd made with the rotation and the bullpen.

Years later, I was watching the show *Lost*, which was one of my favorites. It's about a plane that disappears. And the lead actor, Matthew Fox, plays this guy Jack Shepard, who is from Boston. And one of the captors on the island tells Shepard: Since your plane crashed, Americans reelected George W. Bush, Christopher Reeve died, and the Boston Red Sox won the World Series.

Jack started laughing so hard that he was crying. He didn't believe it. So the captor pulls out a TV, and my voice comes out of it, saying: *"Red Sox fans have longed to hear it: The Boston Red Sox are world champions!"*

Jack stood up and leaned toward the TV, stunned and over-whelmed. Watching that with my daughters was really cool.

Without really planning to, I was steadily moving away from the job that had defined my life, even when I was a child: the Cardinals play-by-play announcer. In 2005, I cut the cord completely. I left the Cardinals for good.

I wasn't doing many of their games at that point. I had gone from a full-time Cardinals announcer to a half-national, half-local guy to a national guy who did ten Cardinals games a year, just to keep my hand in it, which was silly. I couldn't do the job justice. I was supposed to keep up with the Cardinals like I was a regular announcer, even though I wasn't. I felt like I was keeping my hand in it to say, "I'm part of the Cardinals broadcast team," and it made no sense. You can't do ten games a year and be part of the Cardinals broadcast team. It doesn't work like that. Cardinals games have to be the number one thing in your professional life. That's how it is for Dan McLaughlin, who is the TV play-by-play guy for the Cardinals. I wanted to get out of his way. It's not right for somebody to drop into the booth ten times a year and act like it's his job.

By the end of my time doing local TV for the Cardinals, I would leave my house at 6:15 P.M. for a 7:10 game. I was one traffic jam away from not making the first pitch. That does not speak well of me at all. I realize that. When I started, I would get to the park three or four hours before the game. For a FOX broadcast, I show up four hours before the game. It was ridiculous for me to leave my house at 6:15 P.M.

I had mentally moved on, and it wasn't fair to the Cardinals or to the other people doing the games.

I owe the Cardinals so much, and I will always be thankful for the time I spent doing their games. And I know that I will be identified with the Cardinals the rest of my life, no matter where I go. This amazes me: A lot of people around St. Louis still think I do their games. They don't pay that much attention. You think they do, because it's St. Louis and the Cardinals are so big, but a lot of them really don't.

Sometimes, somebody will come up to me on a Tuesday in July and say, "Doing the game tonight?"

I think, "No, I haven't done the game for ten years."

That's not how they think. They see me, they think of my dad, and they think of the Cardinals. And of course people in other cities often feel the same way. I still hear "You're on the Cardinals payroll, you're obviously biased." I got tired of hearing it, which was another reason to get out of there and go my own way . . . but I still hear it.

Leaving the Cardinals was the right decision for me. Most people in my business would agree that being the number one baseball and football play-by-play guy for FOX is a better job than local baseball. I'm certainly fortunate. But *better* is subjective, and *better* does not mean "better in every way." My dad was fairly well-known among sports fans throughout the country but beloved in St. Louis. Me? I'm on everybody's TV. But I'm not beloved like that anywhere, and I never will be.

Chapter 12

Married . . . with Children

When you're on TV a lot, you never know who is watching, or what they think you can do. Some viewers think I should do some rather obscene things to myself. Peter Lassally, a producer who worked with Johnny Carson and David Letterman for many years, wanted me to be a guest host for *The Late, Late Show* on CBS. I was flattered. Craig Kilborn had left, and CBS had not settled on a replacement. FOX had no problem with me hosting a show on a rival network for a couple of days, which is one more reason working for FOX is so great. The FOX attitude is "As long as you do what we pay you to do, we don't really care what you do with the rest of your time. Just try not to get arrested."[31]

---

31. Just make sure you always refer to FOX in all caps.

CBS did not have that attitude. Lassally had to fight to get permission for me to guest-host the show. I was flattered he wanted me enough to use some of his pull to get me.

I always thought my dad should have gotten an opportunity like that. People often (and understandably) compared my dad to other great baseball broadcasters: Vin Scully, Harry Caray, Mel Allen, Red Barber. I always thought he had qualities in common with another legend: Johnny Carson.

My dad was quick on his feet and could deliver a funny, unrehearsed line in response to somebody. Even though he grew up in Massachusetts, he had this Midwest, everyman kind of attitude. Carson was from Nebraska. David Letterman is from Indiana. David Hill, my boss at FOX for many years, said that what made Carson great was his Midwest sensibility that everybody seemed to relate to. My dad had that as well.

I decided to give the talk show a shot. I hosted for two nights, and I learned a few things:

1. I could do a monologue. You can tell yourself you can do it, but you don't know until you go out there and have to make the audience laugh. We also did a couple of funny skits. At one point, I walked outside the studio, which was next to the studio where *The Price Is Right* is taped, and joined the people waiting in line for our show. I pretended to be annoyed because I wanted tickets to see *The Price Is Right*, and asked the people in line if they had any idea who this "Joe Buck" guy was. Nobody knew.

2. Hosting a daily show is *hard*. It's not hard like pushing a tractor up a hill with blisters on your feet, but still, it's hard work. The show may be an hour, but you can't just show up ten minutes before it starts and leave when it ends. I was working with Kilborn's writers, and we ran the show the same way he did. I would arrive at eight thirty in the morning and leave between seven and eight at night. It gave me an appreciation for how hard guys like Letterman had to work, even though they made it look easy.

3. I did not want to host a daily talk show. It was fun, and I thought it went well. I interviewed Ludacris, Kristin Chenoweth, Jason Patric, and Adam Scott.[32] Jason and I did this Shakespeare-style reading from his movie *Speed 2*, which had flopped, and it was hilarious.

But I found that hosting the show wasn't as exciting as doing network TV sports. I had just done play-by-play for the Super Bowl. That's an adrenaline rush. Going from that to a daily talk show was not that appealing to me.

Afterward, Lassally told me, "If David [Letterman] got hit by a bus, you're the guy that I would want to take over." Clearly, he did not

---

32. We're getting into heavy name-dropping time now. I swear there is a point to it all. To make you feel better, here is another embarrassing story about me. I was once the emcee for a Budweiser wholesalers' meeting. Tim McGraw was giving a concert. I was supposed to bring him a Bud Light in the middle of his song, "I Like It, I Love It." So I brought the beer, and he put the microphone in front of my face so I could sing the next line. But I didn't know the next line, so I just pushed the mic back in his face. Brutal!

want Letterman to play in Manhattan traffic. But it was really nice of him to say.

My mom and sister called after they saw me on *The Late, Late Show* and said nice things. I called Ann and she was dead asleep. She never watched it. I think she was worried that I would want to do something like that full-time, which would mean moving out of St. Louis. That notion really scared her. My world was increasingly in New York or Los Angeles. St. Louis is such a provincial town. I started to feel like everything had to fit into a little neat box in St. Louis, so people can kind of know what you're about before they even really know you. But it was also our hometown, and Ann had no interest in leaving.

I didn't really want to leave either. I loved St. Louis, and I loved my job. I just wanted to share the experience of hosting a late-night show with my wife, and we didn't. We never talked about it. We were starting to drift apart.

One night in 2005, I met Paul Rudd for a drink in New York City. He said, "We're going to grab Christina Applegate on the way and we're going to go to this bar downtown." They had just been in *Anchorman* together. So we picked her up, and the three of us were hanging out. Christina's assistant was there, too. At one point, Rudd was talking to somebody else, and it was just me, Christina, and her assistant. We all hit it off.

We ended up over in the corner of the bar playing a video trivia game. I realized that Christina and I had similar senses of humor.

Beautiful woman. Funny. Seems to enjoy talking to me.

Hmm.

I don't think you could describe the conversation as "flirting." But it's fair to say I was smitten. It felt like we were in a high school science class together, about to dissect a fetal pig, and I'm not looking at the pig. I can't even smell the formaldehyde. All I can see is her.

Nothing ever happened, but I realized that this was the kind of woman who really excited me. I don't mean physically. She got my mind working. She was fun to spar with—a smart, funny, hardworking woman who understood what it was like to do a job in front of a mass audience.

I went to see her star in a Broadway musical, *Sweet Charity.* I was in a crowd with Steve Horn and Preston Clarke, who was living in New York at the time. I was married, but I was also mesmerized, watching this beautiful, smart, funny actress perform in this musical. And as I sat in that theater, it hit me:

I am my father.

This is what he did. He had a wife and kids. He met a beautiful, smart, funny actress, and he had an affair with her. He married her and started a new family. The difference, of course, was that Christina and I were not having an affair—it was easy to let my brain run wild, but this was clearly a one-way feeling. It was an affair of my mind. She became a friend for the few days that we hung out. After that, I barely ever really talked to her again.

But at the time, I thought, "Man, I don't laugh like that at home with my wife anymore." It hit me hard.

I went home, and that was a tough reentry into my real life. I started to realize that I had the job of my dreams, two beautiful daughters, more money than I had ever dreamed of making, and the biggest house I could conceive. And I was not happy.

I think, for most parents, once you have kids, they become your life. I know there are people who write a child-support check or show up at the occasional school play, and that's it. But for most of us, everything starts to revolve around your kids. You work so you can support them. You get up and take care of them. You spend every day thinking, "What can we do for the kids? How can we make their lives perfect?"

Your relationship with your spouse can become an afterthought. And I think that's a big mistake. But it's a mistake Ann and I made. After feeling that my dad was gone for so much of my childhood, I was determined to give my daughters a different experience. I watched *The Wiggles* and *Teletubbies* with them. I changed diapers. I dropped them off at school and picked them up afterward.

When my girls were young, I would play with dolls with them, making up voices for Barbie and Ken. I would do an impression of Barney the dinosaur to make them laugh. I even bought a Barney costume to wear to a surprise costume party once.

I kept the costume and threatened to wear it when I picked up Natalie and Trudy from school one day. They thought I was kidding. I wasn't. I pulled up in our Volkswagen Beetle convertible in full Barney gear. The woman on the intercom at the school said: "Buck girls, Barney is here for you."

When Natalie saw me, she ran around the corner of the building to hide. Trudy looked at me and immediately burst into tears. They were mortified. I told them that someday, they would laugh about it—and now they do.

Even though I travel a lot for work, I had more time with my kids than most working parents do. When I'm home, I'm home—I'm not in an office from nine to six. And a lot of the time, I would take the girls on the road with me, and they would sit in the back of the booth during a game, like I did as a kid. They knew how to behave. We would see all these great cities around the country. Those are some of my fondest memories as a kid—traveling around the country with my dad. I loved that I could do that with my girls. It's such a cool way to grow up.

I believed that, despite our marital struggles, Ann and I were doing things right with our daughters. We were raising great kids. But the marital struggles were real.

I was a prime candidate to find comfort with another woman. But I was determined not to do it. Whatever my unhappiness was, whatever Ann's unhappiness was, whatever our shortcomings were, I never wanted it to be about somebody else, whether it was Christina Applegate or Jane Smith. It didn't matter. I wouldn't go there.

I knew the pain that an affair could cause, because I lived it my whole life. That was all I saw as a kid, from the moment I was born. It brought heartache to my half siblings that stuck with me forever. My dad had an affair, I came along, and their lives were never the same. I had nothing to do with it. But I still felt like it was my fault. I felt the venom, even as a five-year-old—this weird sense that I had made their lives worse.

And I think back to being on the road with the Cardinals, seeing players who I idolized in a hotel bar and thinking, "Wait. That's not his wife." I knew their kids. I knew those kids' moms. And I knew this wasn't right, but my dad said, "Just put your head down, Buck. Keep walking." *What happens on the road stays on the road.* I didn't want that kind of attitude in my life.

I couldn't live with myself if I hurt somebody like that. And anyway, an affair is kind of an elaborate cop-out. It takes the focus off your own issues and puts the blame on a third party. When a marriage starts to break down, and there's somebody else involved, it just becomes about that somebody else, not the *reasons* somebody else ever got involved.

So I never had an affair. Never seriously considered one. But if you want to mess with your mind, as a guy in a disintegrating marriage, you should attend a three-day fantasy camp with Christina Applegate. It really crystallized some of my marital problems for me.

I would sit in my car outside our enormous house and talk to my mom on my phone, just to get away from the tension. Or I would drive to Walgreens and work in my car there, just to get some peace. I'm not blaming Ann. It takes two people to make a marriage work, and when it doesn't, two people are at fault. There was tension both ways.

I think I realized by 2005 that we were not going to fulfill the whole "'til death do us part" thing. But I still didn't want to get divorced. I didn't want either of my daughters to go through high school in a broken home, with divorced parents.

That's also a pretty common mistake, I think: staying together for the sake of the kids. It's an offshoot of the first mistake: ignoring your relationship with your spouse so you can focus on your kids. You are still saying, even subconsciously, "The marriage isn't important. The kids are." Trudy had *twelve more years* of school at that point, but I was thinking, "We'll stay married that whole time. For her. I'm going to slug it out!" Like "Ah, heck, that's only a decade of my life, plus a couple of years—what's the big deal?" I really think, even after they get married, husband and wife must continue to "date." They have to keep courting each other and find some time to be together, just the two of them. In my opinion, that is key to survival.

I wanted to keep our marriage going and raise the girls together in a household that looked perfect from the outside. It's what pleasers do. If something bad happens, I assume it's my fault. And that's a problem, because you try to make everybody else happy, and the last person you think about is yourself. But if you're not making yourself happy, you can't make other people happy. That's why therapists talk about the speech that flight attendants give: If the cabin loses pressure, you put your mask on first before you assist your child. You need to be right to help them be right.

Still, I didn't fully appreciate all of this at the time. I knew my marriage was falling apart. I tried to block it out and concentrate on the wonderful life I appeared to be leading.

Chapter 13

Buck Rhymes with *Suck*

If you watch sports enough, you probably have your favorite broad-casters. I certainly have mine.

To me, Mike Tirico is as good as it gets in this business. Every time I watch him do a football game, I am inspired to work harder, just to keep up. Mike's preparation across the board is incredible. I probably appreciate it more than the average viewer because I know what goes into it. He doesn't just read the graphic off the screen. He knows it and adds supporting material extemporaneously, with ease. He has such great recall, and such a smooth delivery. You can tell he works extremely hard, yet he makes it seem easy.

And it's not just football. He is beyond great at everything he does. I marvel at his ability to do golf, an NBA game, tennis, football—

whatever is on the calendar. If our country suddenly decided that our favorite sport was feather bowling, Tirico would be our best feather-bowling announcer. If I ran a network today, and we needed to hire a guy to cover multiple sports, I would hire Tirico over anybody else. It's not even close.

Tirico is not the only play-by-play guy I admire, of course. If I needed to hire an announcer to do the NFL, and only the NFL, I would call Al Michaels. He is the best, maybe ever, because he's been able to do it at a really high level for a really long time. He's done it with different partners, on different networks, in different eras, with different audience expectations.

Al is not the funniest guy in the world—he's not that kind of entertainer. But as far as the mechanics of doing a broadcast and being accurate and an enjoyable listen, he is the best. If a catch is made at the 40, and the guy lunges for a couple of extra yards, I might say, "He's across the 40." Al tells you, "He's out of bounds at the 42." It's a subtle difference, but broadcasters notice. He's past seventy now and still as fast and good as anybody. It's so impressive.

And if I needed somebody to give my eulogy on national television, I would call Bob Costas. Admittedly, this would be hard, because I'd be dead, and my cell phone coverage plan does not include calls from the great beyond. But I'd want Bob to do it. He is the best at making a point wisely and artfully. He'll go on Bill Maher and talk about gun violence and hold his own. He's the kind of guy that we all hold up in the sports broadcasting world as if to say: "See? We're not just idiots talking about sports. Some of us can be smart, too."

Bob's memory is phenomenal. My dad hired him at KMOX when

he was basically fresh out of Syracuse. I admire the way his mind works. Mine doesn't work that way. I wish I had his memory. I get the information in my head, I regurgitate it on the air the way I want to regurgitate it, then it's gone. Costas is one of those legends who is even more respected by the people in the business than people outside.

There are a lot of great broadcasters. Those are a few of the guys I admire most.

And of course, if you watch sports enough, you probably have your *least* favorite broadcasters. I have mine, too, though I'm not going to call them out in a book.

In the 2000s, I was surprised to learn that a lot of viewers have one broadcaster they just can't stand:

Me.

I don't emote enough for some people's tastes. People say I seem detached. They say I think I'm above it all. The opposite is true: I never, *ever* want to seem bigger than the game I'm covering. I think people tune in for the game, and the play-by-play broadcaster's job is to present the game. People don't tune in for the announcers unless they are related to them. And I don't have enough relatives to improve the Nielsen ratings.

So when people say I don't emote enough, are they wrong? Well, it would be easy for me to say that. I mean, this is my book, right? I could just call it *Am I Awesome or What?* and rip the people who rip me.

But there is a problem with that.

And the problem is . . . they are not *completely* wrong.

I understand the criticism. Sometimes I listen to old broadcasts, from the mid-2000s, and I think, "Damn . . . that's *boring.*" Still professional, I think. (I hope.) I liked my call of the 2004 World Series, when the Red Sox broke their championship drought: "Red Sox fans have longed to hear it: The Boston Red Sox are world champions!" But sometimes I did not rise to the emotional level that the drama demanded.

How did that happen? Well, there were a few factors. One is, as I mentioned, that I never wanted to seem above the game. I was also very conscious of the fact that I replaced the great Pat Summerall as FOX's top NFL play-by-play announcer. If you grew up in the eighties, Pat will always be the standard. He was a master of underdoing it: *Montana . . . Rice . . . touchdown.* No exclamation points necessary. Summerall was the best ever at saying the most with the fewest words. Just his presence and his voice were enough.

I fell into a trap of trying to sound like Pat. I couldn't help it. Funny thing: I had never actively tried to sound like my dad, even though our pacing and some of our sayings were similar. But I did try to sound like Pat. I guess I figured: *That's how you do it. Who am I to pretend I have a better way than Pat Summerall?*

Also, when I took over from him, I was in a three-person booth with Aikman and Collinsworth. We should probably call it a four-person booth and count Cris twice. I'm kidding, but this is true: Cris is fantastic, absolutely brilliant about the game, and there was not a lot of room in that booth for me to do my thing.

Then there was this: I was so determined to *not* seem like a homer for whoever was winning. That may have led to some flat calls, especially when the Cardinals were involved.

And every time somebody implied I was a homer, it affected me. The worst was in 2006, when the Mets played the Cardinals in the National League Championship Series. Before Game 7 in New York, I was screwing around during a rehearsal on camera—dancing to loosen up the crew. Without asking FOX, the Mets took the video off our private feed and put it on the big video board at Shea Stadium before the game. The crowd booed loudly.

The message was clear: Once a Cardinals guy, always a Cardinals guy. It stung. I wish I could have ignored it, but I'm not wired that way. I was as mad as I've ever been in this business. It was totally unprofessional of the Mets to do that.

That video messed me up—not just for that night, but for the rest of the playoffs. It still affected me eight days later, when the Cardinals won the World Series. My call was way too subdued. I was so worried people would say I was a Cardinals fan that I didn't do justice to the achievement. The Cardinals won their first World Series in twenty-four years. That was a huge deal in a baseball town like St. Louis. My call sucked. I listen to it now and I'm embarrassed. I think, "What a rip-off for Cardinals fans."

Looking back, I wish I had listened to the people who said I didn't get excited enough. I was just so frustrated that people thought I didn't want to be there. I *love* being there. I'd rather work than not work. I love doing a game and trying to put my miniature stamp on it.

Sometimes I watch games and think, "That broadcaster thinks people tuned in to watch *him*." It turns me off. Deep down, I still feel like somebody's kid doing these games. I don't want to overstep my boundaries. If a big moment happens, I try to get out of the way.

The criticism came to a head in Super Bowl XLII in 2008. That was the game when the New York Giants' David Tyree made that ridiculous helmet catch against the New England Patriots. People around the world were screaming because they couldn't believe what they just saw.

Me? I was not screaming.

And you know why? I wasn't totally *sure* of what I just saw.

If you're watching at home, and you say, "Wow, what an amazing catch!" and then the replay shows it was incomplete, nobody cares. If you're doing a game for 100 million viewers and you make that mistake, you look like an idiot. Forever.

I couldn't be sure that was a catch until I watched the replay. And by the time we confirmed it, my instinct was: *Don't be too loud and make it all about yourself.*

So I'll stand by that one. In general, though, I think there was some validity to the criticism. I believe I have a good feel for what's going on in a game. I know when it's a big moment. I just got sucked into a trap of not wanting to overdo it.

But then, when I do it my way, the critics come out in full force. Like in 2005, when the Vikings beat the Packers in a playoff game. I was doing the broadcast with Troy and Cris.

For years, when we did Vikings games at FOX, Randy Moss was the team's biggest star. We would request him for one of our Friday production meetings. That's when a few coaches and players sit down with us to talk informally, off camera, about the game. Those Friday production meetings can be incredibly helpful (when Tom Coughlin or Peyton Manning talks to us) or painfully unproductive (when Bill Belichick sits down with us). But they are generally useful, and most players agree to do them when we ask.

Moss never said yes. Not once. Eventually, you stop asking. This isn't high school, he's not my crush, and I'm not trying to take him to the prom. If a player doesn't want to talk, that's his prerogative. It's really fine. I don't make a big deal of it.

So I had no history with Randy, good or bad. I enjoyed doing his games because he was such an electrifying player. Still, I was surprised when he jogged over to the goalpost and pretended to pull down his pants and moon the crowd in Green Bay. He then appeared to rub his ass on the padding on the goalpost.

In 1981, at age twelve with my mom in an empty TV booth at Busch Stadium, I saw Cardinals shortstop Garry Templeton grab his crotch and basically flip off the fans. Whitey Herzog literally yanked him into the dugout. That winter, Herzog traded Templeton for Ozzie Smith. So when I saw Moss do something even worse, I reacted to the moment the way I would react to a home run or an interception: I said what came to mind.

"A disgusting act," I called it.

Then I said we shouldn't show that again. I didn't merely say it to my producer. I said it on the air. It just hit me that way. It was early evening—certainly early enough for a lot of kids to be watching. Also, I think everybody gets a little more conservative after they have kids.

You go from "Who gives a shit?" to "Hey! Stop that! I give a shit!" You start caring what's put in front of them on national TV.

Moss's actions weren't going to cause me to lose sleep, but I usually give some opinions during the course of the game, and here was one of them. I didn't think what he did was right. It seemed pretty obvious to me.

Well, from the reaction, you would have thought I gave classified information to North Korea. I got ripped as much as I've been ripped for anything in my career. Sportswriter Woody Paige slammed me on ESPN. He called me a hypocrite for doing a Budweiser commercial with an egotistical pro athlete named Leon. Of course, Leon was NOT A REAL PERSON. He also didn't moon paying customers on national television.

Somehow, criticizing a guy for mooning the crowd was worse than *actually* mooning the crowd. Criticism comes with the job, but I still don't understand that one. And there was an implication that the white broadcaster was trying to keep the black receiver from expressing himself. In some cases, it was more than an implication.

I'm not an angry old man. I don't care if a guy does a flip, or pulls a Sharpie out of his sock. I did the game when Terrell Owens took the pom-poms from a cheerleader after a touchdown and started cheering with them. It was funny. (Owens, like Moss, would never meet with us in production meetings, so it's not as if I liked him more than Randy.) Some of that stuff is great. It makes for fun moments on the broadcast. We replay the hell out of it.

But this felt different to me. If you're sitting on the couch with your seven-year-old, why should you have to explain a guy rubbing his ass on the goalpost?

Randy was fined $10,000 for the mooning. That week, a reporter asked him if he had written the check yet. He said, "When you're rich, you don't write checks."

So how would he pay?

"Straight cash, homey."

That was funny. But it didn't end the controversy. Vikings fans were still mad at me. Sometimes fans try to out-anger one another to prove they love their team the most. Once a crowd starts running down a hill like that, it's hard to stop them. Red McCombs, who was the owner of the Vikings, wanted me removed from the Vikings broadcast the next week. People in Minnesota thought I was biased against Randy Moss, the Vikings, the state of Minnesota, snow, people of Scandinavian descent, the movie *Fargo*, all of it. I was the bad guy.

I'm sure it added to the perception that I'm a prude. I'm not. I enjoy a good mooning as much as the next person, when the time is right and the ass is properly sculpted. The time was not right. People defended Moss by saying that Green Bay fans moon the visiting team bus when it arrives. Well, if they all give you the finger, that doesn't mean you can turn around and give the finger to the crowd, either. A player has got to be above that.

To this day, when I go to Minnesota, somebody will bring up the mooning and my reaction. I really learned the power of the word *disgusting*. If I had said rubbing his ass on the goalpost was *inappropriate* or *unsanitary*, the whole thing might have faded by the end of the game.

Does this kind of criticism bother me? It shouldn't. I know that. But . . . well, I'm sure you've heard a million jokes that start something like this: "A rabbi, a priest, and Bill Clinton walk into a bar . . ."

Try this one.

Five people come up to this announcer named Joe Buck.

The first one says, "You do a good job."

The second one says, "I agree."

The third says, "Yeah, they're right."

The fourth says, "I loved that call on the World Series last year."

The fifth says, "You suck."

Who does Joe Buck believe?

If you answered, "the fifth guy," you were correct. For a long time, I couldn't help it. I always deferred to the naysayer.

I wish I were more like McCarver in that way. Tim was the best at dealing with criticism. He dealt with more than anybody I've ever been around, and it started before the Internet. He just didn't ever let it slow him down, and I admired that so much. He was confident that he knew the best way to do his job, and that's how he always did it.

Me? If I checked Twitter or some message board, I'd blow right through the compliments and go straight to the guy who said I'm only there because my father was famous. And it would bother me.

I mean, when you think about it, the whole "dad got you the job" part of it doesn't make a ton of sense. It made sense twenty-five years ago in St. Louis. It doesn't make much sense in the national landscape. Is FOX really going to ask me to call the Super Bowl as a nod to my dad, who never worked for FOX and died fourteen years ago? That's a stretch. It's more than a stretch. It's nonsensical. When my father worked for CBS in 1991, his name couldn't even save his *own* job. How is it going to save mine now?

But when people say I suck, I hear two voices: theirs, and the little one in my head that's saying, "*You're not good enough.*" It's hard to shut those voices out. Criticism just fans the flame of whatever self-doubt any normal person would have. Maybe there are people who are so supremely confident that they think, "I've got this licked. Wait 'til they hear what I have to say next. Everybody will see how fantastic I am." I think those people are psychos. You'd have to be a complete dick, completely unaware of your own relative unimportance on the planet, to think that way.

There is no doubt that being Jack Buck's kid helped me in a lot of ways when I was younger. But it also works against me in one important sense: I was around this business so much as a kid, so I never thought, "Oh, my God, can you imagine if I were ever to make it into a big-league booth and broadcast for the Cardinals?"

I was certainly excited when I did my first Super Bowl. But my dad did the Super Bowl every year on the radio. So I had been around it. The Super Bowl was never a far-off, mystical destination for me. It was never the other side of the rainbow. I always felt like it was a career possibility for me. That was good, because it made me realize what was possible, but it was bad in the sense that I didn't fully appreciate it when I got there. I felt lucky to be there, but I didn't feel like I had accomplished much. I was doing what I was supposed to be doing.

To this day, I don't really believe that I'm worthy of the seat a lot of the time. Whether it's the US Open or an NFL game, even a baseball game, sometimes I'm really guarded about what I say, because I don't want anybody to think I'm taking it for granted.

Early in my career, I was much freer with my sense of humor. Sometimes I would get off a line and people would crush me for it. Phil Mushnick of the *New York Post*, who writes a scathing, repetitive column that should just be called "I'm Angry and Nothing Is Ever Good Enough for Me," would continually write that I was trying to be too funny, which is awful. You shouldn't have to *try* to be funny.[33]

Steve Horn often told me: "Don't always look for other people's approval." He told me that long before Twitter existed. "Do not listen to the noise," he'd say. Many times, he has reminded me that when Vin Scully worked for NBC in the eighties, he wouldn't wait around for some vice president or director of sports broadcasting to tell him he did well. He just did his thing. Your critics may be right sometimes, but you still need to tune them out and do the job.

I was lucky in a lot of ways—to get my job, to have this new network suddenly become an enormous player in sportscasting, and as viewers often reminded me, to be Jack Buck's kid. But I was also lucky that I got into the business before social media existed.

I can only imagine the fallout if I made the same mistake today that I made in 2000. I was doing a game in St. Louis, and something happened on the field that was an illusion. I mentioned Doug Hen-

---

33. You also shouldn't use Phil Mushnick as your measuring stick for funny, but that's another discussion.

ning, a famous magician/illusionist in the 1980s. When I was a kid, my mom and I saw Henning star in *Merlin* on Broadway. He was a pretty big deal. And I hadn't heard from him in a while. I didn't think anybody had.

So I riffed, on the air: "Speaking of illusion, where *is* Doug Henning? You know what? Now that I think about it, maybe it's his greatest magic trick of all time, to disappear from the American consciousness for ten years, and at some point here soon, I know he's going to pop up and say, 'Ta-da!' "

Clever line . . . or so I thought. To my left, I saw Horn shaking his head. I can spot the Steve Horn headshake even if he is standing behind me. And it's never good. I knew, from his reaction, that I had just messed up.

Horn thought Doug Henning had died.

Whoops.

Horn looked it up, to make sure he was right. He was. I wormed my way out of it on the air. I was lucky there was no Twitter at the time. People couldn't excoriate me. These days, if you make a comment like that, the Magicians' Guild starts picketing your games, which is actually not that bad, because you can't see them.

Twitter does not help. Every time you crack a joke or step out of the normal line of conversation, you're asking to get whacked. Social media kind of brings out the bully in everybody. People write stuff on Twitter that they would never say in person, or even in an e-mail.

It's part of the deal, and I understand that, overall, I have a great gig. But I think this trend is bad for the fans, too. I think about this sometimes: With every passing year, fans' memories of my dad get polished a little more. It's not just him. It's Harry Caray, Pirates broadcaster Bob Prince—any of the greats from their generation. We remember them as wonderful announcers, and we should, but we forget that our expectations were different then. They had freedom to be themselves.

An example: Once, my dad and Mike Shannon were describing a ceremony at home plate before a Cardinals game for a radio audience.

My dad said, "Well, you can see, Mike, by the looks of it from up here, she's Canadian."

And Mike said, "How do you know that, Jack?"

And my dad's answer was "She's big north of the border."

And they laughed at his tit joke and went on to the next thing. There were no protests by the National Organization for Women. Talk show hosts did not play the clip over and over in an attempt to set records for fake outrage. If somebody had a complaint, they had to either call the switchboard at KMOX radio or sit down and write a letter. Somebody would open the letter, say "Huh," and throw it in the trash. And that would be the end of that.

Can you imagine the reaction if I commented on a woman's breasts during a broadcast today? I wouldn't get to finish the inning. That's OK—when I'm doing a game, I'm happy to keep all breast-related thoughts to myself. But it's part of a greater trend, and I don't really like the trend.

Broadcasting has been great to me, so I hope this does not sound like a complaint. It is an observation. But I think people want more from their broadcasters—more flair, more humor, more personality. And yet as soon as somebody says something that is opinionated or not politically correct, they get crushed. And that keeps them from saying anything interesting.

I grew up in a time when Howard Cosell was different from everybody else. He would express his opinion on *Monday Night Football*, and everybody knew, including Howard: Some fans hated him. Some fans loved him. But in the end, everybody wanted Howard Cosell talking about their team.

Now even the mildest comments bring some heat in return. Not long ago, I was doing a game when Johnny Manziel was a rookie. Manziel came in with all this hype as a Heisman Trophy winner, but he was playing poorly. When we came back from a commercial break during my game in Seattle, I mentioned that Manziel had gotten his first NFL start earlier that day. I said something like "Well, my name is Johnny Manziel. You probably know me as Johnny Football. I made my first start today for the Cleveland Browns, and my quarterback rating was 1.1."

Somebody told me the clip went "viral." I don't really know what that means. Do you treat the comment with medication? Anyway, people were talking about it like I said something crazy. It was such a mild comment. I mean, the guy walked out on the stage at the draft doing his little money sign, and then he got his chance to play, and he was terrible by NFL standards. It was just a funny way to say it. I was getting ripped for being too harsh.

This is not just a problem for sports announcers. It's political figures, athletes—anybody in the public eye. My dad would not have been the same Jack Buck with these same politically correct handcuffs that are on everybody. Harry Caray once said on air that he was getting shot up with cocaine, and his broadcast partner said, "You mean Novocain?" and they laughed about it. That's how it *should* be. There used to be a way to say something and then laugh about it and let everybody know it was just a light moment, without being pilloried.

Now you get a fifteen-year-old who can shred you on Twitter for saying something that he or she doesn't like—and might not even understand. The best broadcasters used to have an edge to them, a sarcastic sense of humor. In today's world, I'm just not sure that they would have the freedom to be themselves. These days, even if you have thick skin, your bosses might not. David Hill and Ed Goren didn't need Twitter to tell them what was good. They worked off their gut.

People read the conversation on Twitter or Facebook and panic. So everybody, consequently, is straight down the middle, and anybody who takes two steps to the left or the right sounds insane.

After so many years in this environment, I have developed filters in my head. It hurts me in my personal life. I can be hypercritical of myself. I think, "How did that just come out of my mouth? Will somebody be upset by it?" I'm so conscious of perception that it makes me kind of a social freak.[34]

Then when I have a couple of drinks, I'm like, "Fuck it, who cares? Nobody cares." Then I say whatever comes to mind. I go too far the other way, but it's the only time I can truly relax.

The solution, obviously, is to become a raging alcoholic. I'm kid-

---

34. I bet we would sell more copies of this book if we called it *Joe Buck: A Social Freak*.

ding. But I do wish I could cut loose a little more without worrying about how people will react.

It's hard to find that balance. I understand that if you're constantly searching for all of the public's approval, you're never going to get it. If you're looking for other people's validation, you're just going to be constantly searching and never be happy. But for a long time there, I was searching a little too much.

Sometimes, you don't have to look online to find a critic. Sometimes he is right there in your face, in his office, in the middle of the World Series. This happened to us in 2006, when the Detroit Tigers faced the Cardinals.

Our high-definition cameras caught Tigers pitcher Kenny Rogers with a smudge of a brown substance on the fat part of his thumb on his pitching hand. Ed Goren was in the back of our truck. He said, "What's on his hand?"

It appeared to be pine tar. So we talked about it on the air. A few Cardinals players heard our broadcast in their clubhouse. They came down and told their manager, Tony La Russa. He had the umpires check it out. Rogers wiped it off. He wasn't kicked out, and the Tigers won the game.

The next day was a travel day. When we arrived in St. Louis for Game 3, we walked into Tigers manager Jim Leyland's office.

Leyland was usually very helpful. He is also genuinely funny. This time, he was in no mood to joke. We sat in that office, and it was like a funeral parlor. He wouldn't even look at us. We were trying to make small talk. The series was tied 1–1. We asked about how his trip to St. Louis went.

He said, "Fine."

OK. He was giving only one-word answers.

Eventually, Tim said, "Jim, is there something wrong?"

This was the opening Leyland wanted.

Leyland said, "I'll tell *you*. Was there something wrong? You should fucking know better, Tim McCarver. You played this game. You fucking played this game! You know that these guys have shit on their hands. It's this time of year. You should know fucking better.

"But you know what? FOX doesn't want us in the World Series, Major League Baseball doesn't want us in the fucking World Series. They want a New York team. They don't want the Detroit Tigers in the World Series.

"Of all the people in this room, you should fucking know better. That's not something you fucking talk about."

To Tim's credit, he stayed calm and poised.

Tim said, "Jim, that's not right. If it's on there, people are talking about it. It's my job to talk about what we see. It's not my job to cover it up." He also explained that FOX had no problems with the Tigers being in the World Series.

Leyland said, "That's fucking bullshit. What are your questions? Let's go."

We got out of there quickly. It wasn't like Leyland was going to calm down and start giving us good answers. But the most telling part of the conversation was not what Leyland said. It was what he did before he said it:

216

He left his office door open.

That way, his players could hear his rant.

I think it was all manufactured so his players would see him standing up for them. It was, as Jim Leyland himself might say, fucking bullshit.

At the end of that World Series, when it was over, Tim said, "I'm going to go down and talk to Leyland." That was not usually his style. Normally, he would bolt after a game.

I went with Tim down to Leyland's office.

Tim said, "Look, I know you're pissed off about what happened in Game 2. But I just want you to know we're just trying to do our jobs. I'm trying to do my job the best I can, and you're trying to do your job the best you can. You guys have had a hell of a year. Thanks for all the time you gave us. Good luck. Have a good off-season."

It was a classy move. Leyland was fine at that point. They had just lost the Series in five games. It was over. I think the stress was gone.

We started doing that a lot—visiting managers after a series. There usually isn't any controversy to address—we just thank them. These managers do spend a lot of time with us. They give us a lot of information that they don't give everybody else. We want them to know it's appreciated.

That same fall, James Brown left our pregame show, *FOX NFL Sunday*, to work for CBS. I was asked to replace him. But there was a problem. *FOX NFL Sunday*, as you might imagine from the name, is broadcast on Sundays. So are my games. And I could not be in two places at once.

I was presented with two options.

Option Number 1: Quit the games. Steve Horn thought this was a good idea. His argument was that if I got more face time on TV, I would be in a more prominent position. But I didn't want to give up the games. The games are why I got into this business in the first place.

Option Number 2: The pregame show, which had been shot in a studio in LA, would go on the road with me. Some people take an extra carry-on bag when they travel. I would take Terry Bradshaw, Jimmy Johnson, and Howie Long.

This was not my idea. But David Hill thought it would be like ESPN's *College GameDay*, with fans at the stadium holding up signs and screaming behind us. So that's what we did—we took *FOX NFL Sunday* on the road that year, which was an enormous expense.

And honestly: It didn't really work. NFL games are not like college games. People do not show up hours beforehand, hoping to get on TV. We had a lot of empty parking spots behind us. It was more like a *College GameDay* rehearsal than the actual show.

And the pregame guys—Bradshaw, Long, and Johnson—wanted no part of being on the road. They liked staying at the same luxury hotel every week, getting picked up in the morning, doing an hour-long pregame show, halftime shows, postgame stuff, and getting out of there. They weren't real interested in going to Minnesota one week and Kansas City the next, just to do the show in front of empty parking spots. I couldn't blame Terry, Howie, and Jimmy for feeling that way. They were so great to me, but I knew they didn't like the setup.

We started losing audience share to CBS for the first time in a long time. Our producer told me people missed James Brown. He said I needed to smile more. *Great—I lost weight and got hair plugs, and now I need to worry about my teeth?* I was also told to tee up these other guys more and not really have an opinion.

I said, "Well, it's not my fault that James Brown left. I wasn't involved in that negotiation. And this is me. This is who I am. You asked me to do this. If it's not good enough, it's not good enough. But I'm not going to be fake."

I wasn't allowed to do much on the show. The pregame show was scripted, which baffled me: Why go to such lengths so I can be involved if I have to read somebody else's words? So I would play my little role, and at the end of the show, I would hop into a golf cart and race to the broadcast booth. It hurt my chemistry with Troy because I wasn't spending much time with him. I was basically just showing up before kickoff.

After the game, I had to sprint down and do our postgame show, *The OT*. And that went better, because you couldn't script it. We had to react to what happened that day.

Thankfully, my agent, Marvin Demoff, had put in my contract that at the end of the year, I would have a choice: be the studio host or do games. For the last two weeks of the season, we did the pregame show in Los Angeles at the FOX NFL studio and I didn't do any games. But I had made my decision: I would give up the studio job and stick with the games.

While I was in Los Angeles, Jason Patric invited me to a New Year's Eve party at Naomi Watts and Liev Schreiber's house. Jason had remained a close friend after our 2001 hangover wore off.

I don't know about you, but I don't get invited to Naomi Watts's house very often. I was not actually invited this time, either. But Jason got me in, and I brought Steve Horn, who *definitely* doesn't get invited to Naomi Watts's house very often.

Perry Farrell from Jane's Addiction was there, and so was actress Gina Gershon. I was in heaven. You can fill a room with Wayne Gretzky and Michael Jordan and guys like that, and for whatever reason, I don't flinch. Maybe it's because I've been around famous athletes my whole life and I'm used to it. But give me a room full of Gina Gershons and that's fun to me, because I enjoy their work and I love talking to them.

After we left Naomi Watts's house, Jason said, "Kate Hudson has a New Year's Eve party at her house."

I said, "Are you sure we're invited to this thing?"

He said, "Yeah, yeah, we're invited."

"So how did you get invited?"

"My publicist."

"OK."

So we walked in the front door. It was like 1:00, 1:30 A.M. The paparazzi were packing up. I was walking in, thinking, "God, the last person I want to see is Kate Hudson. She's going to say, 'Happy New Year! You're nobody. Get out!'"

She answered the door. She said hi to Jason and gave him one of those big fake Hollywood hugs.

Then she stopped me and said, "Wait. Who are you?"

"Uh, I'm with Jason. Is it OK that I'm here?"

She said, "You're the football guy! You're the football announcer!"

She grabbed me by the hand. She and a friend of hers, Juliana Roberts, sat with me and talked for the majority of the rest of the night.

Kate and I really hit it off. And she is a *huge* football fan. We have been friends ever since.

The following year, before the Giants beat the Patriots in Super Bowl XLII, I ran into Kate and her dad Kurt Russell, on the field. My wife did not object to my friendship with a beautiful Hollywood star, partly because I never told her. Our marriage was already crumbling. Even though Kate and I were just friends, I thought it would be easier to avoid the topic altogether.

But that night, after the Super Bowl, I ate pizza with my family and I said, "You know who I met today? Kate Hudson. She was great. Couldn't be nicer." It was a full-on lie—I had known Kate for a year, and we had become good friends. I don't know why I chose that moment to tell my wife I had just met Kate Hudson. But if you believe there is a benevolent God who covers the asses of men who tell stupid lies to their wives, then he was looking out for me, because the next day, we all ran into Kate at a private airport.

Kate ran up to me and gave me this big hug in front of my wife and kids. Steve Horn said afterward, "That seemed a little too familiar." But as far as Ann knew, that was the first weekend I met Kate. My relationship with Kate somehow featured the lies and awkwardness of an affair, but without any of the sex.

And as my marriage fell apart, I relied on her friendship to help me get through it. I learned that Kate is a genuinely good person. She is very sweet, but also funny and cutting, and she is very smart. She's a great mom. She's driven. She's accomplished.

But she's also somebody's kid. She will forever be known as Goldie Hawn's daughter to some people, especially people my age. The younger generation probably doesn't even know what a great actress Goldie Hawn is. But Kate has had to live with that her whole life.

We've talked a lot about following in parents' footsteps. You feel like you're constantly trying to prove yourself because your famous parent gave you a head start. You're constantly fighting that perception, and you even have to fight it in your own mind.

At some point, the nepotism charge doesn't fly. These aren't desk jobs, where you can be the Vice President of Doing Nothing, and everybody else in the office cleans up your mess, but nobody will fire you because your father owns the company. I'm the one who has to do the game. Kate has to act on-screen. Either you can do it or you can't.

Just as broadcast booths were my playgrounds when I was a kid, Kate has been on movie sets her whole life. She was around her mom, and then she was around Kurt Russell a lot—Kurt is technically her stepfather, but Kate thinks of him as her dad.

I've told Kate what I can't tell many people (though, obviously, I'm putting it in this book) . . . I appreciate when people say they loved my dad, because I loved him, too, but it can be frustrating to always hear compliments that start with "I got to tell you, your dad is the greatest I've ever heard." Sometimes I wait for the second part, the acknowledgment that I do the job well, too, and most of the time it doesn't come.

Somebody will come up to me in the airport and say, "Your dad was the best."

I'll say, "You bet he was."

Then they walk away to buy a nine-dollar airport muffin, and all my old insecurities creep up and park themselves in the front of my brain.

I think it's inherent in everybody's human nature to think, "That person got advantages that I didn't get. And that's why that person is successful." It doesn't even matter if you are in the same line of work. I just think that's just the way people are. When you're on the other end of it, it can prey on your insecurities.

Here I am, in my forties, and I've done a lifetime's worth of World Series and several Super Bowls, but I feel no different inside than I did when I started as Jack Buck's kid. I still look at players as if they're older than me, which is hilarious. I'm older than all of them. I'm older than some managers. But I don't feel like I am, because I still see myself as a kid around these big-league ballplayers. Emotionally, I can't turn that off.

I will sit in a production meeting with Aaron Rodgers and I feel like he's a contemporary, but he isn't. I have to remind myself that he's fourteen years younger than I am. And Aaron Rodgers probably doesn't even know who my dad was, or if he does, he isn't thinking, "That's Jack Buck's son. That's the only reason he is here." But I feel that's always hanging over me.

Nobody really wants to hear this, of course. In the big picture of my career, and my life, this is all a very small price to pay. I get that. But it can still mess with my head. I think the lesson is that, no matter how lucky you are (and I am certainly lucky), you're still going to have challenges and tough days.

And if those challenges are a result of being a celebrity, the only people you can really confide in are other celebrities. Everybody else will think you're a prick with no perspective. During the 2008 World Series in Philadelphia, I was getting off a hotel elevator when I ran into Eddie Vedder. I didn't know him, but he's a sports nut—probably a bigger sports fan than I am. So we talked for a minute outside the elevator. I'm a huge Pearl Jam fan, so the next night on the broadcast, I mentioned that they were playing the last concert ever at the Spectrum, which was about to be demolished. We have been friends ever since. He has really helped me deal with the criticism that comes with my job.

I think Kate understands it better than anybody. She told me once: "Americans love a good success story. They're just not sure what to do with the success story that comes out of a success story."

In two sentences, she summed up one of the essential conflicts of my life.

Part 6

The Bottom

Chapter 14

Grandstanding

In the spring of 2000, my family flew to New York for the Sports Emmys, where my dad was scheduled to receive the lifetime achievement award and I was scheduled to lose.

I was nominated in the play-by-play category against Bob Costas, Al Michaels, Dick Enberg, and Mike "Doc" Emrick. They were all legends. I was thirty-one. Nobody thought I would win, including the presenter, boxer Floyd Mayweather, who opened the envelope to announce the winner and said: "*Joe Buck?!?!?*"

Mayweather was as shocked as I was. For years, that was the closest anybody came to knocking him down.

Our table erupted. I collected hugs from my mom, my dad, my wife, Ann, and my best friend from home, Preston. What timing!

They were only there because of my dad's award, and then they saw me win my first Emmy. I accepted my award from Mayweather, then went back to our table and got ready to present my father with the lifetime achievement award.

Per Buck tradition, I introduced my father with the best speech I could give, and then he blew me away. He was shaking because of his Parkinson's disease, but of course he just used that to make people laugh.

He told the crowd when he shook hands with Muhammad Ali, it took a half hour to untangle them. He thanked the Frenchwoman who saved his life during World War II by hiding him in her basement—"and that was in Cleveland, Ohio." He boasted that he was now the only person in the world who had Parkinson's, diabetes, a pacemaker, vertigo, eight kids, and an Emmy.

This was the man St. Louis had known and loved, always ready with a line. I once gave him a big hug and a kiss on the forehead at Busch Stadium and he said, "Be careful, Buck. Not everyone knows we're father and son."

After my father's Emmy acceptance speech, executives from multiple TV networks told me they had no idea he was so funny. They meant it as a compliment, but it was bittersweet for me. I thought: "*Really?* You had no idea? Well, then, shame on you for not listening. He made rain delays as much fun as games. He brought the house down with speeches for charities for fifty years. He has *always* been this funny."

But to them, he was a play-by-play guy. That's it.

My father never told me this perception bothered him, but I think it did. I think that's why he took his shot at *Grandstand* with Bryant Gumbel in 1975. He wanted to be more than just a play-by-play guy.

So did I.

And when I got my chance, I jumped at it.

The call came from Ross Greenburg of HBO Sports in 2009. He wanted to do a show that would lead into *Pornucopia* or *G-String Divas*. Well, those were not his exact words. Bob Costas had just left his HBO show, *Costas Now*. Ross wanted to create a show that would replace Costas, with me hosting.

And I'm actually a big fan of *Pornucopia* and *G-String Divas*. And *Cathouse*, too. It's good stuff in a pinch. Here was my big chance to have a show on the same night on the same channel, and nobody was asking me to take my clothes off. (Thank God for everybody.)

Costas was doing serious work—special interviews with baseball legends, that kind of thing. I love Bob. No veteran broadcaster has been better to me in my career. When I started broadcasting, and everybody was saying (with some justification) that my name got me the job, Bob spoke up and said some very nice things. He gave me credibility. That meant the world to me.

So Bob is great. But we're very different people. He's a measured, thoughtful guy with an intelligent take on almost everything. I mean, whether it's gun control or the suicide squeeze, he's got an opinion and it's well thought-out.

Me? I'm loose. I like to goof around. I like to wing it. I was a guest on Costas's HBO show once, and my appearance says something about the difference between us. Before I went on, he had author Buzz Bissinger and *Deadspin* founder Will Leitch on, discussing the role of new media in society. It was supposed to be a serious discussion, and it quickly got a little *too* serious. Bissinger lost his shit. He read something from *Deadspin* on the air, quoting some commenter who had the screen name Balls Deep.

Honestly, *Deadspin* and sites like it scare the hell out of me, with their screen-grabs of announcers in mid-blink and their way of finding out what happens when the camera turns off. But Buzz acted like Leitch had just eaten his puppy.

When I came on for my segment, I sat down and asked Costas if he would refer to me by my screen name, Balls Deep. I had cleared the line with Steve Horn in the dressing room first. If Horn had said no, I probably wouldn't have done it. But he knew Costas, and he knew the line would work with him. And it did.

So in my mind, the one thing I knew about my show is that it would be different from Bob's. We would not host town meetings or fireside chats. We would not try to ease tensions with North Korea. We just wanted to entertain you before the boobs came on.

And this seems obvious now, but it wasn't obvious to me then: You can't build a show based on what it's *not*. That just doesn't work. You need a vision. That sticks with me as I look back on my frustrating experience on *Joe Buck Live*. The other thing that sticks with me: When I think of our debut, I don't think of it as *Joe Buck Live*. I think of it as *The Artie Lange Show*.

I sort of assumed people would beg to be guests on an HBO show, especially after I assured them I would keep my clothes on. As it turned out, I had to do the begging. I basically had to book the show myself, which was not what I expected. It was OK, though. Whatever I had to do, I would do.

The first guest I booked was Brett Favre. He had just retired. I guess I need to be more specific with that: He had just retired from the Jets. The year before, he had retired from the Packers. There were rumors he would come back, but he hadn't talked to anybody.

I had to work hard to get that interview. I'm not used to that. We get spoiled at FOX—for an NFL game, we arrive a few days early and the coaches and a few players sit down with us. It's all prearranged.

I planted the seed with Brett early. I massaged it over time. I said, "Whatever it takes to get you to New York on this night, I'll do . . . and if you can, don't talk to anybody before you show up that night." He was great. He said he would do it, and he didn't talk to any reporters before our show.

I arranged for a private plane to pick up Favre in Mississippi and fly him to New York.[35] I asked Brett if he would come back to the NFL, and he said, "I am considering it." Then he talked about his health, and said he'd been in contact with the Vikings, and by that point in the Favre retirement saga, everybody in America could read between the lines: He would play for the Vikings. There it was on the ESPN ticker, before our show was even over: *Brett Favre tells HBO's Joe Buck Live* . . .

Then we had Michael Irvin and Chad Johnson (formerly Ochocinco) on for the next segment. I asked Chad about calling out his quarterbacks, and he told me to give an example. I didn't have one.

---

35. HBO never reimbursed me for it. Ross, if you're reading this: Check or wire transfer is fine.

Oops! I had never done a live interview show before, and I learned a lesson there: If you challenge the interviewee on anything, you better be able to back it up.

But other than that, I thought it was going well. You have to understand: We didn't do a pilot or a dry run. I believed I could host a show like this, but I had never done it. And most of the way through our first show, I felt good about it. I think the audience enjoyed it, because the rating was great throughout the show. But for the next week, nobody would be talking about the rating for *Joe Buck Live*. It's the only time in my TV career where ratings didn't seem to matter. All anybody talked about was Artie Lange.

I realize that whatever I say about this episode may smell like sour grapes. I hope not. I just want to explain what really happened.

I should say, up front, that having Artie as a guest was my idea. I'm a huge fan of the *Howard Stern Show*[36]—when I used to drop my daughters off at school, I would turn the radio to Howard as soon as they closed the car door. Artie's humor was one of my favorite parts of Stern's show. I know how brilliant he is, and he is a big sports fan.

So I suggested we have Artie as part of a panel, which would be the third and final segment. I also invited Paul Rudd. Paul had become a big star, and it's been fun to see that happen for him, and for our other friend Jon Hamm. When we were all hanging out at nineteen or twenty years old, who could have predicted it?

---

36. My biggest hope for this book is that it helps me get invited as a guest on Stern's show.

Rudd has been successful in his career almost from the beginning. He appeared in the movie *Clueless* when he was in his twenties and blew everybody away. Hamm had a longer road. He was a waiter in both St. Louis and Los Angeles. He slept on Preston's couch. At one point, he came back home to St. Louis to teach drama at his old high school. He went back out to try acting again.

Hamm was on TV a little—an episode here, an episode there—and he had supporting roles in some movies, but he was still looking for his big break. At one point, he told me, "I'm going to read this show on AMC. I don't know who watches AMC. I'll give myself another eight months. If nothing really clicks, I'm going home. I'm going to get a job."

The series, of course, was *Mad Men*. It changed his life. The funny thing is that all the qualities that made the Don Draper character so great were apparent when Jon was in high school. He was a stud—so smart, remembered everything. He just was a cut above. You could tell even then.

Anyway, I invited Rudd, and I also asked Jason Sudeikis, whom I knew through Rudd. So it was me, Rudd, Sudeikis, and Artie Lange. Artie was the only guest HBO booked that night. I booked the rest.

Before the show, I went into Artie's dressing room.

I said, "When you go out there . . ."

He said, "Hey, man, thanks for having me on. This is fucking great. I'm a huge fan. I was a big fan of your dad's."

I'm thinking, "Well, this is going to go well." Then I said, "When you get out there, just light me up, make fun of me, have fun. I don't care. I can handle it. Not a big deal. Let's just make this different."

This was one of the reasons I wanted to do the show in the first place, to let people know I don't take myself that seriously.

Artie seemed like the perfect guy to tweak me. It was right in his wheelhouse. Unfortunately, he also keeps liquor and assorted drugs in his wheelhouse, and he snorted Vicodin and drank Jack Daniel's before he came on the show. (He has since admitted this in his second book.)

When people are high, I don't notice. My radar for that doesn't exist. I learned that over the years. Other people say: "Man, that dude is so wired on coke." I'm like, "What? Do you mean I shouldn't have given him my car keys?" I'm oblivious to that stuff.

I was vaguely aware that Artie did not seem quite right. But the idea that he might be stoned out of his mind did not register with me.

Artie hijacked the segment. I said something tongue-in-cheek about TMZ being my favorite website, to set a light tone, and I asked Rudd a question, and then we turned to Artie . . .

"Joe, TMZ is your favorite website? What is your second one, SuckingDick.com?"

Well, *that* was a pretty sharp left turn. But the crowd laughed, and I laughed. And when he got that laugh, he just went off. He called Tony Romo "Tony Homo" and said Jessica Simpson looked like Chris Farley. I tried to steer the conversation toward Sudeikis, but Artie wasn't going for it.

At one point he did compliment me. But most of what he said was just off. I wanted a good ribbing and he was attacking. He said, "Sorry to ruin your fucking great show." He started imitating my dad. He tried lighting a cigarette, which made me really mad. (Odd, I guess, since my dad smoked for years.) We didn't have a clear vision for the show, but it sure wasn't *that*.

Do you think ten minutes on a treadmill feels like a long time? Try sitting out there, looking into the crazed eyes of Artie Lange, stuck.

I was thinking, "I have no way out of here." I mean, if I lose it—if I get mad and jump down into the pit with him—where does that get me? First of all, I'm not going to win a battle of wits with Artie Lange. He is too funny. Second, if I start getting really vulgar or dirty, I lose everything I've built up in the other parts of my career.

I couldn't say, "Yeah, I went on SuckingDick.com and I saw your mom's picture there! Hahahahahahaha! Everybody, please forget that joke when you see me doing the World Series!" Plus, he was high, so he would always take the insults further than I wanted to go. I just had to sit there and take it.

I felt like the crowd turned on him after the second or third joke. It went from "Nice line!" to "Wow—that was pretty mean." But he didn't notice because he was so out of it. And it became really uncomfortable in the room.

When the show mercifully ended, I had to walk to the center of the stage and say, "Good night from New York!" You know, like the last ten minutes of the show had not happened.

I was not mad at Artie. Truly. Sure, he was over the line, and it was tense and awkward, but I had *asked* him to make fun of me. I couldn't really get mad at him for doing it. I was just disappointed, because I thought the show had gone well to that point, and now all anybody would be talking about was Artie.

Little did I know: The people in charge of the show were about to wimp out.

My wife was there. My kids were there—they heard everything Artie said about their dad. And before I could get off the stage, HBO Sports's media relations guy, Ray Stallone, let a group of reporters rush the stage and start asking me questions.

At that point, I had not seen Ross Greenburg. I hadn't seen my family. I couldn't even go to the bathroom. I couldn't get off the stage. And these reporters came up. I always try to be respectful of journalists and their work. When I read an interesting sports story and discuss it on the air, I always try to mention the writer's name. I think they deserve that recognition. But I was not quite ready for reporters to ask me questions in that moment.

Richard Sandomir of *The New York Times* asked me: "Joe, do you feel like you just got cornholed on national television?"

What? Can you even get "cornholed" into the austere pages of *The New York Times? In the wake of his uncouth exchange with Mr. Lange, Mr. Buck denied feeling cornholed.* I was like, "No, I don't feel like I just got cornholed on national television. Thanks for asking!"

Another reporter (a stringer for the *New York Post*) asked if TMZ was really my favorite website. I could see where this was going, and I didn't like it. So I got out of there. Greenburg came out from behind me, behind the stage, and started going off on Artie: "He will never be on HBO again! This was a travesty! This was insulting!"

So then it became HBO versus Artie Lange. And everybody assumed I was on HBO's side, morally offended by Artie, curled up in the fetal position, crying and kissing my Jack Buck bobblehead doll. In reality, I was more disappointed by the reaction of HBO.

Come on, guys! This is HBO! It's not *Meet the Press* or the *700 Club*. I wasn't happy with what Artie did, but the show was over—we couldn't *un*-broadcast it. I wanted HBO's people to talk about the ratings, which were strong. I wanted them to have fun with it.

I was used to working for David Hill at FOX, and he would have handled it completely differently. David is kind of a maverick Australian guy. He would have said, "There you go, folks! There's the first episode of this *live* show! Tune in next time! Who knows what you're going to see?" But I think HBO Sports people take HBO Sports so seriously, you're not really allowed to have fun like that.

I had hoped the show would give people a different side of me. Instead, Artie's appearance gave them ammunition to rip me. New York radio personality Mike Francesa devoted a big portion of his show to blasting me. This is a guy who has fallen asleep on his own show! At least my show kept him awake.

Howard Stern talked about Artie's appearance at length on his next show. All the guys were ripping Artie. That's how bad it was: *Howard Stern* thought Artie crossed a line.

When you start a new show, you usually need some time to find your rhythm, to see what works and what doesn't. We were suddenly being talked about *too much*, and for the wrong reasons. It would be hard to recover.

I called Artie, and as you might expect, there was an apology. But the apology was from me to him, for HBO's reaction. I left it on his voice mail.

Artie called back two minutes later. He felt terrible. He said, "Look, man, I'm just a comic. I got that first laugh and I went overboard. I never want to get in the way of a person making a living. That wasn't my intent." I had to convince him I wasn't mad at him. But I really, truly wasn't.

I wanted to have Artie on the next episode. I thought that was the only way to go—otherwise, we would look scared and embarrassed about what happened.

But Ross's position was "Absolutely not!" God forbid we offend the people who tuned in early for soft-core porn.

I said, "Ross, you've got to hear me out. That was *me* onstage. Not Ross Greenburg. Me. You don't know me very well if you think that I can't laugh at myself, or I can't make light of it to try to win people back. I *have* to talk about this."

He said he would think about it.

Then he called me back and said, "OK."

I said I would write something fun and tasteful to open the show with Artie. There would be no mention of SuckingDick.com or its partner websites. Everybody would laugh and we could put the whole thing in perspective and continue with the show. Ross agreed.

I called Artie. I said, "Here's what we're going to do."

He said, "Great. I'm in." I think he was eager to make amends, too.

And about four days later, Greenburg called me back and said Richard Plepler wouldn't allow it.

"Who's Richard Plepler?" I asked.

"He runs HBO," I was told.

Artie Lange had been banned from the network. Forget it.

Ross said, "Not only are you not allowed to have Artie Lange on, you're not allowed to reference it on the second show."

That was ridiculous. There was no way I could walk out on that same stage and act like Artie's segment never happened. I would look like the same sensitive, weepy, self-important weasel that some people think I am.

I told Ross if I couldn't talk about Artie, I would quit. I meant it.

As much as I wanted the show to work, I didn't need it. I had my job at FOX. I was in a good place.

They huddled to discuss it. I was hitting golf balls at Old Warson Country Club in St. Louis to get the frustration out. I was dreading having to disinvite Artie. I might as well call him and say, "Artie, why don't you go on Howard's show and rip me for an hour? By the way, I'm hitting golf balls at a place called Old Warson. Go use that to destroy my manhood, too."

Plepler thought the ordeal was over.

"Nobody cares," he said. "It's under the pavement."

But I cared. I wanted to talk about it.

On a three-way call, Plepler decided, "All right, we'll do it your way. But it had better be done right. It better be funny."

No pressure there. But I didn't really care what they thought anymore. I had to do it.

So I wrote this opening:

I'm walking through Times Square, checking my phone and not paying attention, and I bump into somebody. I look up, and it's Artie. He does this John Belushi thing, like he is so excited to see me. I give this "Oh shit!" smile, like I just ran into the mob boss who doesn't know I am sleeping with his girlfriend.

Then I turn around and start running through Times Square. He runs after me.

We shot it. As Artie chased me, his pants started falling down, which was not intentional. He was losing weight at the time and the pants were just too big. But that made it funnier. The studio audience loved it. Artie was on the show for less than a minute, but the skit did the trick: We had addressed it, laughed at it, and moved on.

After the show, Ross came to me and said, "That was the right thing to do. That was well done." I was so pleased—not because it was a funny segment but because I stood up for myself and made a bad situation better.

To this day, I walk into stadiums and people yell, "Artie Lange!" When I got a Twitter account, it seemed like every fifteenth tweet was about Artie. People seem to think I'm mad at him. The truth is that we've become friends. I wrote the foreword to his book. I have nothing bad to say about Artie. He's a good guy who has demons, and he did what he thought I wanted.

We did two more episodes of *Joe Buck Live*. HBO said they canceled it because another show went over budget and they had to cut something. The ratings for the second and third episodes were strong, and I'm still proud of the show.

In retrospect, it was a mistake to have a live show with no clear vision. The live-TV aspect never bothered me. I *like* live. I do live every week of my life. So I wanted that show to be live . . . but looking back, *Joe Buck Taped* would have saved me from the Artie fiasco. If we weren't live, it would have never been on the air. That's one of the reason they tape those shows. Those things are edited all the time.

I wish we could have kept going and really made it a great show. No show can hit its stride in three episodes. Think of Letterman, or Fallon, or Conan after three shows—you just can't know what the style of the show will become. We never got the chance.

Chapter 15

The Split

In 2009, I went back to Indiana University to speak to a pair of telecommunications classes at the request of the dean of the school. I hadn't been back there since I left to take the Cardinals job in 1991. For the first time, mammoth Indiana University felt small to me. It was good to be back. I remembered being a freshman, trying to remember my Social Security number and hoping nobody would burn down my dorm with a hot pot.

I was there to be interviewed for a Big Ten Network show that focused on Big Ten alumni. I sat onstage in the IU auditorium, and the director of the National Sports Journalism Center there, Tim Franklin, interviewed me. He asked about my dad, my childhood, and my career. I had never really taken stock of it all before. I just kind of lived my life. But as I sat up there and talked about my life, my work, and my kids, I almost broke down in tears.

I flew home and I got into bed. It was almost midnight, and I told Ann, "Well, let me tell you about this show we just did."

She wasn't interested. To be fair, she had just gone on a trip with her girlfriends, and I wasn't interested in hearing about that. So we went to sleep. That said a lot about our relationship.

And the times we did talk, it was tense and uncomfortable. Sometimes we fought, which really bothered me. I didn't like the idea that my kids were constantly confronted with fighting. I had not experienced that growing up. The fights never really escalated into all-out screaming matches, but there was constant tension in the house.

I felt it. The kids felt it. I'm sure Ann felt it.

I was terrified of getting separated because I didn't want to tell Natalie and Trudy. I'm sure that's why a lot of couples stay together. Inertia takes over. Who wants to take the energy to move to another house? Just suck it up and keep going. It was always easier to let another day, another week, another month, or another year go by than to actually start the process of possibly getting divorced.

But I started to realize: We were staying together for the kids, but it wasn't a good environment for them. They were better off if we were apart.

If my girls were in this same situation as married adults, I would be heartbroken for them. But I would also want them to have the courage to do what they needed to do to be happy. I would never want them to stay in an unhappy marriage.

So I moved out.

I never harbored any ill will toward Ann. She and I raised two wonderful girls together, and I wish her only happiness. It just became clear to me that we were not going to experience happiness together again.

Moving out did not end the stress, of course. I was physically breaking down. I went for a physical early in 2010, and I was falling apart. My vital signs were all over the place. My blood pressure was high. My cholesterol level was up. My weight was down. I weighed 180-something—60 pounds off my peak, and certainly less than was normal for me when I'm feeling healthy. I was so thin that people thought I was sick. I liked the idea of being thin, but it wasn't for the right reasons. I was stressed and not eating.

I felt it was my responsibility to make everything right for everybody, and I couldn't make it right for *anybody*. And it was a hard thing for me to admit, but I was powerless. I couldn't fix it.

My doctor was like, "Man, these were really different readings than we've ever had for you." Ann was with me. I was just sitting there with my head down, thinking, "This has got to be it. I'm going to die."

I really leaned on my sister, Julie, at that time. We have gone from combative coexisters to best friends. She took over as the female in my life with my kids and organizing my office when I was gone working. She has loved my girls like they were her own.

And more than at any other time in my life, I missed my dad. I wished I could have talked to him. If I could have brought him back once, for one day, that's when I would have done it. It wouldn't be to talk about broadcasting Super Bowls or World Series. It wouldn't even have been to talk about my mom or my sister or my kids.

I wanted to know what it was like when his marriage was falling apart—what he regretted, what he saw from mine, and what he thought was salvageable. After he died, one of his close friends told me that my father foresaw trouble on the horizon for Ann and me. I wished I could have asked him, just once more, what I should do with my life.

Shortly after Ann and I separated, somebody called a sports radio station in New York and said, "I know why Joe Buck is getting divorced. I've heard from a really good source that he's been having an affair with Fernando Tatis."[37]

Tatis had been the Cardinals third baseman a few years earlier. You know what Woodward and Bernstein always said: If a guy calling into a sports radio station says it's true, it must be true. The rumor quickly spread across the Internet.

A. J. Daulerio from *Deadspin* texted me and said, "What's the deal with Fernando Tatis?"

I said, "What are you talking about?"

He said, "Go online. Call me back."

I went online. I don't know what I expected to read, but I did *not* expect to read that a former third baseman and I were redefining "the hot corner."

I thought, "Oh, my God."

I called A.J. back. I said, "The irony of that is, if I *were* gay, there

---

37. This is my least favorite name-drop in the whole book. And half of you don't even know who Fernando Tatis is!

would still be no chance of me sleeping with that guy, because he hates me."

This was true. Fernando Tatis did not like me. I don't know why. I must have said something at some point that ticked him off. When Tatis played for other teams—I'm speaking about baseball here—he wouldn't acknowledge that I had known him from the days when I was calling all his games with the Cardinals.

I'd say, "Hey, Fernando. How are you doing?"

He would look up and walk away.

So for whatever else was going on in my life, I was not sleeping with Fernando Tatis. Or anybody else. I just wanted to get through the divorce, because that's really the best thing you can do: Just get through it. It will never be fun. You just hope it's not worse than it needs to be.

While my marriage was disintegrating, I was involved in a brief, frightening, and (in retrospect) hilarious controversy. It involved Alex Rodriguez, which should not surprise you. Most baseball controversies involve Alex Rodriguez.

I really like Alex. He is much more a baseball historian than people think. He proved that on air during the postseason in 2015 on FOX. He was always really respectful of McCarver, which I appreciated. He made Tim feel good. Alex grew up in Miami, watching the Mets on WOR, a superstation you could watch in South Florida. Tim was the Mets color commentator.

He would tell Tim: "That was the sound track of my summers:

listening to you and [Ralph] Kiner call the Mets games." I don't think he was bullshitting when he said that.

Alex always wanted to be liked so desperately, but he kept stepping in shit every time he left the house. I feel sorry for the guy. I recognize that I'm in the minority. He's really sensitive, and that doesn't work, especially in New York. You can't beg for approval there. You shouldn't even try.

So in August 2010, we were doing a Yankees–Red Sox game (shocking, I know) in the middle of a pennant race. My nephew Jack was with me, and I wanted him to see the field at Yankee Stadium. We walked down there.

Alex was on the field. He saw me and said, "Hey, Joe."

I said, "Hey, Alex," and kept walking.

That should have been it. But then Alex started a conversation: "Is that your—"

He was going to say "son" or "boy." He didn't know me that well at that point. He didn't know I had two daughters but no sons.

He never got the word out, because at that exact moment, he got crushed in the leg by a Lance Berkman line drive. Alex went down in a heap. Then he got up and started hopping on one leg all the way to center field, where he lay down and started rolling around.

Jack looked at me and said, "That's not good."

No shit, kid. I looked around like I'd just murdered somebody on the field at Yankee Stadium. We tiptoed around like John Belushi in *Animal House*.

Somebody said, "Did anybody see what happened to Rodriguez?"

And Bill Hall, the Red Sox second baseman, said, "Yeah, he was talking to that FOX announcer—what's that guy's name? Joe Buck? Yeah, Joe Buck."

Uh-oh. *No, guys, you must have me confused with another Joe Buck!* The story started spreading like wildfire to the nine million reporters up there. Next thing I knew, I was doing an impromptu press conference, with the New York reporters asking, "What happened?"

I said, "I don't know what happened. I'm walking out, he says 'hey,' I said 'hey,' I kept walking . . ."

Rodriguez was scratched from the lineup. *That's not good.* I asked to speak to Brian Cashman, the Yankees general manager. Cashman came up to the press box. I wanted him to know I felt terrible and that I didn't intentionally distract Alex.

Cashman was great. He said, "Joe, if it wasn't that, it might have been something else. It's not your fault. It's OK. We're not mad at you."

I could finally exhale, knowing I wasn't going to get escorted out of Yankee Stadium.

But we had to explain, on air, what happened. Viewers would want to know why A-Rod wasn't in the lineup. I asked Horn for advice. We decided honesty was the best policy. I just told people what happened. Tim backed me up on it. He was always such a good teammate for me.

Keith Olbermann was there, and he asked me what happened, and I explained it. Olbermann wrote on his blog afterward that there were "two versions" of what happened with Alex. One was that Alex turned to talk to Joe and got hit. The other is that Joe shouted out to Alex during batting practice, distracting him, and that's why Rodriguez got hit.

That was bullshit. There were not two versions. It was just a freak thing. I know how to act during batting practice. I've known for my whole life.

I was not a fan of Olbermann anyway. When he does baseball highlights, part of his shtick is mocking my dad. Whenever a runner was obviously going to be safe, Olbermann would say, "They're not gonna get him!" It's a reference to my dad making a mistake in his CBS days. I may be the only person in America who knows who Olbermann is referencing. But I know. It pisses me off whenever he does it.

So I got past that A-Rod incident and the Tatis rumor. But I still had to get through the divorce.

And while I was trying to do that, I went in for hair-plug operation number eight.

And that's when I woke up with no voice.

Chapter 16

Vocal Discord

By this point in the book, you may have forgotten why I'm an idiot. Let me remind you: I had become a serial hair-plugger, and the eighth surgery had cost me my voice. I didn't know exactly why. I just knew I was in big trouble. It was early 2011. With only a few weeks to go before the start of baseball season, my voice was not suitable for broadcasting major sporting events on national television. I couldn't even order a cup of coffee at Starbucks.[38]

I went to see Dr. Bruce Haughey at Barnes-Jewish Hospital in St. Louis, hoping he could perform some magic. Instead, he sprayed "banana-flavored" numbing spray into the back of my throat. (That

---

38. Oh, the horror!

crap tastes horrendous. Bananas should sue.) His scope went into the back of my throat.

After asking me to make a few noises for him, Haughey pulled the scope out and said:

"You have a paralyzed vocal cord."

I would have been very happy to go through life without having a paralyzed anything.

I asked, as loud as I could: "Well, how long does this last?"

The answer will never leave my memory. I can recite it verbatim, I can hear his inflection, and I can recall the unease in his voice: "It could be three weeks, three months, six months, a year, or it could never come back."

By the end of his answer, I could barely remember the beginning of it. I could only hear the end:

". . . or it could never come back."

Never? That's a long time, doc.

At this point, I had three options:

1. Tell the world that I might have blown my career because I wanted hair plugs.
2. Take some time off. I just couldn't bring myself to do that. My dad would have disapproved.
3. Did somebody say *virus*? We have a winner!

I told people my "virus" would clear in a week or two. It was a bold-faced lie. I even lied to my bosses at FOX. But it was the only option I felt I had. I wasn't ready for the ridicule I would receive if people knew what really happened. I was just buying time.

A paralyzed vocal cord is actually on the list of warnings they give you before general anesthesia. (Read it next time you go under!) Mine probably got paralyzed because of the cuff that the surgery center used to protect me. One doctor[39] (who was not involved in the operation) later told me that during the six-and-a-half-hour operation, the cuff probably got jostled and sat on the nerve responsible for firing my left vocal cord. After a few hours of being squashed, the nerve said, "That's it. I'm done."

I don't know if stress contributed to the problem, but I suspect it did. I was months into divorce proceedings.

I arrived at a FOX seminar in early March and acted like I had a cold. I literally needed a PA system to be heard in the banquet room. I cannot imagine what my bosses must have thought as I squeaked and hissed out words. But I bet they were *not* thinking, "Well, at least his hair looks great!"

At one point, I was playing golf in a member-guest golf tournament down in Cabo San Lucas, Mexico. Matthew McConaughey was there. You look at Matthew and see a great actor. I look at him, and my hair-plug detector starts beeping.

I don't think McConaughey has ever talked about getting hair plugs. But I've examined Before and After pictures of McConaughey. I know good work when I see it. And his is *fantastic*. Whoever moved his follicles should perform live in front of a studio audience.

So, even though we were on the golf course, I decided to go fishing—for information. I told McConaughey what happened to my voice, with the hopes that, as a fellow connoisseur of the hairscaping arts, he would tell me who did his work.

---

39. Dr. Steven Zeitels. You will meet him in these pages shortly.

Instead, he just said: "So what you're telling me, buckaroo, is you fixed your video, but you fucked up your audio."

I laughed for the first time in a long time.

I started to realize I was a prime candidate for antidepressants. I started taking Lexapro to relieve my anxiety. My failing voice wasn't just a professional problem. I struggled to be heard when I ordered food at a diner or talked on the phone. I became obsessed with my vocal quality.

I tried everything. I did fake play-by-play calls for my daughters when I drove them to school. I did exercises to retrain my cords. I could not break ten seconds without gasping. I also had to say words with the long *E* sound over and over, because those are the hardest with one cord. *Each . . . Easter . . . easy . . . eek . . .* over and over. I sucked at that, too. How the hell was I going to broadcast a baseball game? What if Derek JE-ter committed an E-6?

Dr. Haughey, a brilliant doctor in his own right, selflessly referred me to a doctor in Boston named Steven Zeitels. Dr. Zeitels could go down my throat with a long needle and inject my sleeping vocal cord with Restylane, a fillerlike substance—and he is one of the few surgeons in the world who could do it while I was wide awake. Getting a needle shoved down my throat, like getting a needle shoved in my scalp, was never on my bucket list. But neither was getting fired, so I was ready to try it.

Dr. Zeitels has fixed some famous voices: Adele, Steven Tyler, Roger Daltrey, James Taylor, Dick Vitale, and Doc Rivers. You walk into his office and see signed pictures from these music and broadcasting giants. I must say: I took solace in those photos. These people were so pleased with his work, they wanted their pictures on his wall, announcing to patients: "You are in the best place you can be." I suppose it was possible that he bought the photos on eBay and forged the signatures, but that seemed unlikely.

If the Restylane didn't work, we were looking at a permanent procedure that involves GORE-TEX being inserted surgically, to hold the paralyzed vocal cord in place. The problem with that is that your airway is cut in half, and breathing can become difficult.

I kept thinking of worst-case scenarios. Not being able to breathe was definitely up there.

I tried another kind of treatment, too: old-fashioned relaxation. I went back to Cabo, figuring I would do yoga, then rest and try to get my voice right. I brought two books with me. One was *A Prayer for Owen Meany*[40] by John Irving, which I had read years earlier and I wanted to reread. The other was *In the Garden of Beasts* by Erik Larson.

As it turned out, I could have brought all the Harry Potter books and the Bible printed in six languages and it wouldn't have mattered. I got there and found Pat Perez, the PGA Tour player and a friend of mine. Within two hours we were drinking margaritas out on the golf course and having a ball.

By the end of the week, I was more tired than I was when I got there. I was about to go back to work, which would normally be exciting for me, but I was scared because of my voice.

---

40. First line of *A Prayer for Owen Meany*: "I am doomed to remember a boy with a wrecked voice." Perhaps my subconscious chose to bring it to Cabo.

We went to this dinner party. I was sitting at a dinner table with one of my best friends, Mark Human. And this guy came up to Human and said, "You know, the house manager made pot brownies."

I had never tried marijuana, in any form, ever. I never wanted to do it. I had a close friend in college who smoked a lot of pot. Whenever he did it, I got out of there. I don't like the smell of it. I don't like being around it. People in an altered state make me nervous and uneasy. I always want to be in control.

But as I sat there in Cabo, I had already lost control of so many things.

I looked at Human and thought, "You know, maybe that's what I need."

I never smoked anything in my life. But now I wouldn't have to smoke it. It wouldn't affect my lungs or my vocal cords. It's a brownie! We put them in lunch boxes! How bad could it be? Maybe it would make me relax for the first time in two years.

I ate it. Human had one, too, as a show of solidarity. Half an hour went by, and I felt nothing. I was thinking, "Only me. Only I can eat a pot brownie and *still* not relax."

Human said, "Well, let's eat another."

So I ate another. We got a ride to a bar in downtown Cabo. On the drive, I was looking down at my phone, trying to text, and the letters started coming off my phone into my face. I don't remember buying *that* app. I freaked out.

I'm sure stoners get used to that feeling. But it felt like *Alice in Wonderland* to me. We walked into this bar, which was crowded, and I panicked. I wanted to stay in the car. I was convinced—*convinced*—that everybody in the bar:

A. Knew I had eaten a pot brownie.

B. Gave a shit.

They were almost all younger than me, and presumably have seen more interesting things in their lives than a fortysomething sports announcer who was stoned. But I felt like I was fifteen years old again and got caught smoking weed, even though when I was fifteen, I never smoked weed.

I started to lose feeling in my extremities. I felt like I was walking through molasses to get to my seat. *Great. Now my vocal cords AND my legs are paralyzed.*

I turned to this Australian security guy. He was with the Australian version of Navy SEALs. I assume they go on assignment, killing bad guys and stealing their beer. He was drinking a Coca-Cola.

I said, "I need to drink that right now, and then we need to leave."

He said, "Yeah, no worries, mate. We'll get out of here in the next fifteen to twenty minutes."

I said, "No, no, no. We need to leave *right now*. You're going to have to help me get up and we're going to need to go."

He was like, "OK."

He knew I was serious because I was panicking and sweating very seriously. There was no enjoyment in any of this. I was so miserable.

We got up. He had his arm around my shoulder as I walked down these stairs. I went to the right. He said, "No, let's go this way." He pulled me and spun me around. I passed out on cobblestones in the marina, with my head under the rope, almost in the water.

Two waiters and the owner of Nowhere Bar, Pablo Marrone, were standing over me. They hoisted me up moments after I went down and asked if I was OK. I went from foggy and not feeling my legs to hypersensitive to everybody around me. *Did somebody take my picture? Are people tweeting about this? MY CAREER IS OVER.* That's how big a worrier I am. Can you imagine Al Michaels falling down at a bar? I thought I was done.

I was already worried about my career even before I ate that brownie. I walked back, thinking, "Holy shit, fuck, fuck, fuck, I'm dead, this is it, my career's over."

I got home and woke up at 7:00 A.M. the next day. I kept googling my name all day, just to see if I was on some gossip site. I had my sister scouring the Internet. You can imagine this getting out, and me releasing a statement saying this was a one-time incident, and of course nobody would believe that. It would also give FOX an excuse to fire an announcer who couldn't speak anyway. I went out and played golf, just to get out of the house. Nobody ever wrote about it. They either didn't notice, didn't give a shit, or both.

In July, as I continued to struggle to speak, viewers and some critics were writing about me, and not in a good way. One of our PR guys at FOX, Dan Bell, told a reporter, "For as much as Joe has done for FOX, he deserves more time."

He was trying to defuse the situation and defend me, because Dan is a friend who does a great job. But that's not how my warped mind read the comment. I read: "The clock is ticking, Silent Joe!"

I was terrified. I'd been doing games and was struggling. I was ready to quit. I was supporting a lot of people: my kids, Ann, my mom, my sister. I pay Steve Horn. There is this little community of people who are important to me, who need me to be employed. And I felt like they were all screwed.

I also felt guilty because I was still lying to my bosses. I continued to tell everybody at FOX it was a virus.

I was on Jimmy Fallon's show that year leading into the All-Star Game. I remember going in there with Preston Clarke. We were in the green room, doing the prep. I told Fallon that before games, sometimes I sing Johnny Cash's "Ring of Fire" into a microphone that's open to the whole crew to loosen everybody up. I was still doing it with my voice kind of screwed up as it was. I ended up singing "Ring of Fire" with the Roots on his show.

It's amazing how your mind can tell you that things are OK. I came out of the Fallon interview thinking, "Wow, that was really good." I can't even listen to that Fallon interview now. There are so many things I know I wanted to say, but I couldn't say them quickly because I had to gather this big breath to just get something out. It's painful to watch.

You know you're not having a good night as a talk-show guest when the lead guest is Snooki, from *Jersey Shore*. But she was. During my segment, I kept going back to Snooki, making jokes about her being the more important guest, but a lot of the jokes didn't work because I was struggling for air. I sounded terrible.

I was taking singing lessons from a woman in St. Louis, trying to do all these vocal exercises. One evening, I sat in an empty section of Citi Field before a Mets game in prime time on FOX, listening to my iPod, doing scales as best I could. I was trying to warm up my voice to get any movement in there whatsoever.

As you might imagine, if you can barely talk, you can't sing. But I was trying. Normally, I can sing pretty well. I sang in high school. I am my mom's son, and I can hit notes. I carry a decent tune. And when I wasn't able to do it well, that frustrated me, too.

I felt, internally, like I was getting better. But you couldn't hear it yet. When I do a broadcast, I hear where I want to go before I say it. If I hear where I want to go, and I know I can't get there, I'm just trapped. And it forces me to really dumb down what I want to say.

I went to see Dr. Zeitels periodically through that summer and into the fall. Every three months he would give me a shot. He's not a bedside-manner guy. He's a strict clinician who will give you the bare-bones facts. He deals with a lot of thyroid cancer, a lot of lung and throat cancer. He delivers the worst possible news to people. He sure wasn't going to sugarcoat mine.

He had told me when I first went to him: "If you don't get it back within three months, what you have then is probably what you're going to have." Now here I was, six months out and it was the same.

I'd go up there, sit, and they would do the whole banana-spray thing.

"No, it's not moving," he'd say.

Every time I heard that, it was like a hammer to my chest. I kept looking in his eyes for some glimmer of hope. I didn't see one.

Sometimes I would turn to Steve Horn in the booth before games, or even as we were in a commercial break, and say, in my raspy voice, "I can't do this." And he would say, "You're fine. You have a big instrument. If parts of it aren't working, you have enough to get by. And you're more than just your voice." I didn't always believe him, but he knew what to say.

Somewhere along the way, Horn became more than an editorial consultant for me. He became a life consultant. He has ridden shotgun through every moment of my life since 1996. In my life, just like in the booth, Horn sees things that most people around me wouldn't see—or if they did, they wouldn't say it. He is the one who told me to stop doing local car ads on TV in St. Louis because my career had moved beyond that. It was a good point. You don't see Al Michaels or Bob Costas doing stuff like that.

Horn is a wonderful human being and easily my closest friend at this point. Naturally, this means I want to kill him sometimes. That comes with best-friend territory. We are together every weekend. Sometimes I feel he is crowding me, or that he gets heavy-handed. We have screaming fights that would scare the crap out of whoever was in the next room in the hotel. But I rely on him so much, in so many ways.

I went to the All-Star Game in Phoenix in July. The day before the game, I had lunch with David Hill. We were joking around—David was the kind of boss who loved to joke around. But at one point, we stopped goofing around, and he said, "I know you're struggling."

He wanted me to do yoga to help me relax. He had been through a divorce himself, and he knew I was going through one, and he knew that couldn't help my physical condition.

Then he said, "I just want you to know: I don't care if you have to take a year off, you're still going to be my guy here at FOX."

That was a tremendous gesture, and I appreciated it. It took a bit of the pressure off. But at the same time, I knew: I still had to get better. At some point, it's over. You can either do the job or you can't.

I thanked David. But I still didn't tell him what really caused my vocal problems. It was too embarrassing. My career was hanging in the balance, and I was stuck in a lie about my mystery virus, and I didn't know how to fix either problem.

Major League Baseball made me come to the stadium at 9:00 A.M. the day of the game to practice the pregame introductions, where all the players line up on the foul lines. I was trying to save my vocal bullets, but I had to do this. We ran through it, and then I hear: *We have a problem.* The fake players they hired to run out there when I say their names messed it up. We had to start over. *Let's do it again.* Crap.

When we were done, I went out and hit golf balls for a mental break, because I was about to have a nervous breakdown. Then I went back to my hotel room. I had Trudy, Natalie, one of Natalie's friends, and my sister, Julie, with me.

Trudy, who turned twelve that year, wrote me a card. It read, *Good luck tonight. I know you're going to be perfect. Nobody will ever know you have a problem. We're rooting for you.* She stuck the card in my scorebook.

I opened the scorebook when I got to the game and found the card. I cried.

That gesture was so typical of Trudy. She is a pleaser (like I am) and a problem solver, and she always seems to know the right thing to say.

As we got ready to go on the air that night, I was nervous. Tim was nervous. I didn't know if I could squeeze these words out loud enough to be heard. And then, out of nowhere, ESPN's Chris Berman walked into our booth.

Chris said, "Hey, can I talk to you?"

"Yeah."

He said, "I just want to say, I know you're dealing with a vocal thing, OK? I had laryngitis once. Just remember this: We're not as young as we used to be."

I thought, *OK . . . ?*

I have no idea why he said that, or what he thought was causing my vocal problem. Maybe he figured I was smoking too much crack or something. I don't know. But he was trying to be supportive, so I appreciated that.

I rehearsed the pregame introductions a few times. I made notes on the pages. Then somebody from Major League Baseball said they made another change. They handed me a new script, but one page of it was missing. I found out the hard way—as I was introducing them live.

So Miguel Cabrera was standing there, and I said, "From the Texas Rangers, Ian Kinsler." The camera was on Cabrera. I quickly ad-libbed: "Or maybe from the Detroit Tigers, Miguel Cabrera." I didn't know who would appear next on camera because I was looking at the script. I was struggling like hell to even speak these names out and a page was missing.

I thought, "Oh, my God. I'm going to have to go off sight. I hope I get them all correct." If I got the names wrong, people would assume I was an idiot. Nobody would care about the script or the pages missing.

I got through it. People were tweeting: *Is he dying? . . . He sounds like shit . . . He has no emotion . . . This guy sucks . . . I hope he has cancer.*

Believe me, I had *plenty* of emotion. I just had no ability to express it.

During the game, reliever Heath Bell sprinted in from the bullpen and slid into the mound. I tried to make light of it, but I couldn't. My voice wasn't there. It's hard to laugh at a joke from a guy who sounds like he has emphysema.

We had Chris Rose interview Justin Timberlake, who was in the bleachers. He kept saying, "What about that Joe Buck? He's the best. He's the best." People thought he was ripping me, because my voice sounded like crap. The reality is that he was having some fun because we are friends. I got to know him from Kate's party at first in 2006, and then we ran into each other again, and we played golf down in Cabo.

I was not going to say, "He was just kidding, folks! We're actually friends!" If I do that, I'm the asshole who tells the whole world he knows Justin Timberlake, and half the people watching wouldn't be-lieve me anyway. *You're friends, huh? I bet you are. Right. Shut up about your famous friends and call the game in a normal voice, loser.*[41]

We got into the end of August, the beginning of September, and it was hard to pretend everything was OK. Eric Shanks, one of my bosses, called me and said, "Look, I need you to level with me. Do you think you can do the postseason?"

I mustered up the strength to say, as loud as I could, "Yes, I know I can. I'll be ready."

---

41. As we have established, I saved the name-dropping for my book.

That was a lie, too. I didn't know. But FOX trusted me. The one thing I knew from going to Dr. Zeitels was the more I used my voice, the more my vocal cords would swell from usage and the better I would sound. The swelling puffed both cords up like the Restylane shots did to my left cord. So I was getting a little benefit by overusing it.

My voice got a little better in August and September. But it wasn't better *enough.* Put it this way: Nobody would have hired me to do a big game with that voice. I was doing it because I had been doing it for so long, and FOX had faith in me.

Conveniently for me, the Cardinals made the World Series that year, which allowed me to do some home games in the playoffs. My voice was slowly getting better but still wasn't really back. Before World Series Game 2, I walked into the Cardinals radio booth. I'm not really sure why. But it was almost like a mini reunion, because Mike Shannon was there, and so was his daughter, Erin. She had gone from the cute girl in the back of the booth to a doctor of holistic psychology and energy medicine.

Erin said, "I can help you."

She had been reading about my issues. She had taken up energy healing when her mother was dying of brain cancer.

Erin believes that, if you have a balky knee, she can feel it by touching your knee. I mean, it's *out there.* But I was willing to try some stuff that was out there. I would have injected cat urine into my cheeks if somebody told me it was going to help my voice get better.[42]

---

42. This helped me understand why some players use PEDs like human-growth hormone to get back on the field. When you can't do your job, you get desperate.

Erin started working on my throat, rubbing my neck and my throat as I sat there, focusing on my "chakras," or energy points.

I really believe it helped. Maybe it just reduced stress. I don't know. But my voice was steadily coming back. I was still struggling, and it sounded a little bit thin, but it was passable. I sounded more like me.

The series was tied 1–1 and was moving to Arlington, Texas, across a parking lot from where I had broadcast the Super Bowl with a clear voice just ten months earlier.

I said, "Are you coming to Texas?" I didn't know if she was traveling with her dad. I was going through a divorce. She was going through a divorce. People saw us together, and she was rubbing my neck. It was enough to start a rumor in our big old small town that we were together: Jack Buck's son and Mike Shannon's daughter. It would have been the St. Louis baseball equivalent of Julie Nixon marrying David Eisenhower, except that it wasn't true. Erin is like my sister. There was never even a thought of that.

As it turned out, Erin was not planning to fly to Texas. So I got her onto the FOX charter, and she continued to treat me.

I felt better every day. I felt relief on two fronts: I could keep my job, and I didn't have to come clean about what had actually happened. (Until now.)

By Game 6 in St. Louis, I was really feeling like myself. That was good, because it turned out to be one of the best baseball games ever played. It would have been an awful viewing experience if I hadn't had my voice.

The Rangers led the series 3–2, and they led the Cardinals 7–4 in the eighth inning. The Cardinals scored once in the eighth and twice in the ninth to tie it, 7–7. The Rangers took a 9–7 lead in the tenth, but the Cardinals scored twice in the bottom of the tenth. It was wild.

Then, in the bottom of the eleventh, the Cardinals' David Freese hit a game-winning home run to force Game 7, and I knew what to say:

"We'll see you tomorrow night!"

I tried to say it with the exact inflection my dad had two decades earlier.

Serious baseball fans knew it was a reference to my father's famous call of Kirby Puckett's home run to force Game 7 in 1991. I had actually said, "We'll see you tomorrow night!" once before, in 2002, a few months after he died, when the Giants blew Game 6 of the World Series against the Angels. But this was different. It fit just perfectly because it was in St. Louis, David Freese was a St. Louis kid, and it was Game 6 of a World Series that forced Game 7. It was twenty years later, almost to the night.

Not long after the Freese home run, I was with my daughter in a mall in St. Louis. We walked into an "art" store that had some sports memorabilia in it. We walked in because we had a few minutes to kill while we waited for a movie. There was a cool canvas of Freese's follow-through. He had signed it, and he had written: *We Will See You Tomorrow Night. Joe Buck.* That's really the only time a player has acknowledged one of my calls like that.

I didn't plan to say it. It was kind of bouncing around back there in the back of my head. I was reading the outfielder. I saw the outfielder's shoulders slump, and as he turned, it just came out. I don't know how. It's not as if I was planning on a St. Louis kid hitting a home run to force Game 7. But that call turned into one of the most popular of my career. For me, it meant I was back.

I was nominated for a Sports Emmy that year. I had a weird personal history with the Emmys. The first time I was nominated, I assumed I wouldn't win, but I did. Then I won several in a row, and with each passing year, I thought, "Oh, I got this." Then somebody else won, and I felt like an asshole. By 2011, I stopped caring so much.

So I sat in the crowd at the awards show and assumed I wouldn't win. But I did. I appreciated it, because I had recovered from this professional nosedive, and my bosses were there to see me win. But it also told me not to seek validation from Emmys. After all, they gave me one after one of the worst years any broadcaster has ever had.

Part 7

Climbing Up Again

Chapter 17

Happy Days Are Here Again

When I turned forty-four—the same age my father was when I was born—Trudy gave me the most amazing gift. She had seen the old Dan Caesar story in the *Post-Dispatch*—the one that made me cry when I was twenty years old. She took one quote from the article and painted it on canvas:

"Why is a kid, still in college, showing up on what people consider the premier local team network in baseball? The reason is simple, and it's spelled B-U-C-K."

More than two decades later, those words made me cry again. We all try to teach our kids lessons. This was Trudy teaching me. I was devastated by Dan's story when it was published. From Trudy's angle, it was a compliment.

Of course I am lucky to be my father's son. Why run from it?

My girls make me feel so lucky every day. Natalie has a great sense of humor and is not scared to step on a stage. But she is also a deep soul and protector of her younger sister. She is a natural singer and entertainer, and she makes people laugh.

Trudy is so smart and driven that sometimes I wonder if she is mine. She has always been mature beyond her years—some of her teachers have said she could babysit some of the others in her class. I really believe Trudy can win an Oscar and Natalie can win an Emmy. Hey, I'm a proud dad—I'm biased. But I believe that's possible for them. They are far more talented than those they came from. And they can quote me on that when they write their own books someday.

For Father's Day 2015, Trudy and Natalie made me a video. My mom was in it, along with close friends from throughout my life. They gave it to me in Tacoma before I left the hotel for final-round coverage of the US Open. The girls did it and edited it together as a total surprise to me. By the time I finished watching the video, I was a puddle. That was one of my best days as a father.

I worried about my voice all the way into 2015. Now I can finally get through a game without thinking about it at all. It took four years for me to call a big moment in a game, where my voice gets louder and louder, and just do it without that voice in the back of my head saying, *You better not go there, man. It's not going to be there.*

When I got my voice back, I made a decision: I would emote as much as I wanted. I just thought, "Screw it, I'm just going to yell, because I can and I should. These are big moments. I'm not going to downplay them anymore. I'm just going to let it go. If people think that means I'm rooting for the other team, I don't care."

I also decided if I wanted to be goofy, I would be goofy. I've been in this business for twenty-five years now, and in a way, I've been in it my whole life. I should know how to do the job by now, right? It's a lot more fun when you stop worrying about how people will react.

It also helps to be in love.

In the summer of 2012, Troy and I were doing a Broncos-49ers preseason game in Denver. Peyton Manning had just joined the Broncos, and so we spent some time talking about Manning, and also Manning, and Manning's passes, and Manning's move from Indianapolis, and I think we also talked about Peyton Manning.[43]

Afterward, I was walking through the players' tunnel with Steve Horn, Troy, statistician Ed Sfida, and spotter Dave Schwalbe. As we approached the Broncos locker room, a blond-haired reporter was standing against the opposite wall.

I locked in on her from about thirty yards away.

I couldn't keep my eyes off her. Whatever I felt was unlike anything I had before. I *had* to know who that was. I asked Schwalbe if he knew, and he spit her name out immediately. He may have locked in before I did.

"Oh, her name is Michelle Beisner," he said. "She works at NFL Network."

---

43. Peyton Manning, Peyton Manning, Peyton Manning.

I was going through a lot at the time. My divorce had recently been finalized. It was my first year back after losing my voice. I was still trying to figure out how to have a social life, particularly a dating life, with daughters who didn't want to share their dad with anyone.

I immediately put together a list of people who might know if Beisner was married, single, or had recently escaped from prison. I settled on the NFL Network's Rich Eisen, who is a great friend. Like a desperate high school dweeb, I called Rich and asked for a scouting report. What was she was like? What is her dating status? Is she well liked at the NFL Network? I stopped just short of begging for her Social Security number and home address.

Rich told me that she was a great woman, liked by all. She had no airs about her. She was just sweet and really cool.

He said he would tell her I was asking about her. And he did. But, because he is Rich Eisen, always looking for sources of amusement, he made it a game. He told Michelle that there was someone at another network "in the booth" who was interested. But he didn't say who it was.

She said she was flattered but was living with her boyfriend of four years in Los Angeles. Then Rich asked if she wanted to know who was interested.

She rattled off a list of whoever came to mind. She went through a lot of names: "Aikman? Costas? Michaels?" How about Curt Gowdy, Michelle? Oh, wait, he's dead.

Then she finally said: "Please don't tell me it's Joe Buck."

Rich had to inform her that it actually *was* Joe Buck.

"Why would you say that?" he asked. "He is a great guy and a good friend of mine."

She said, "I don't know why I said that. I have never heard any-thing bad about him. He just seems a bit arrogant and smug."

Rich did not tell me her *entire* response. He left out the last part. He just told me she was living with her boyfriend.

I'm kind of amazed I didn't walk away at that point. I have never been the most confident person when it comes to dating. But some-thing told me I just had to meet her.

I wore out Rich's cell phone asking for any detail he could give. I saw former NFL Network reporter/host Kara Henderson at a Rams game (Kara was engaged to Rams general manager Les Snead) and I figured she might know something. I tried my best not to sound like a serial killer as I asked whether Beisner's relationship was stable. When you are chasing something, it seems natural to ask ridiculous questions of people who can't answer them.

I was so desperate for an answer—and not just *an* answer, but the answer I wanted to hear.

As far as Kara knew, Michelle was taken. That was *not* the answer I wanted to hear.

In October, the Cardinals were playing the Giants in the National League Championship Series. Game 1 was on a Sunday night in San Francisco. Coincidentally, the 49ers were hosting the New York Gi-ants in the feature game on FOX. The execs at FOX hatched this idea: I would do Niners-Giants at Candlestick Park at 1:00 P.M. Pacific, then take a streetcar to AT&T Park for the evening MLB playoff game at five.

After all that time when I could barely hear my own voice, I would do two games in one day. I was excited. I felt like Deion Sanders, who once scored an NFL touchdown and hit a major-league home run in the same week. I'm guessing Deion would not buy that comparison. (And I didn't mention it to McCarver—Deion once dumped a bucket of ice water on him.)

In the afternoon, I was in the booth a couple of hours before kick-off and looked down.

There she was.

The siren of the sidelines.

The Aphrodite of the AFC!

(OK, I'll stop.)

I picked up a pair of binoculars for the first time in seven years just to watch her demeanor on the sideline. *She is laughing! She laughs. SHE IS A LAUGHER. Laughing: What she does!* She was smiling as she did her work. Upbeat! Happy! Nice! Within forty-five minutes, she was up in the press box at Candlestick.

Candlestick was great for TV cameras—I can still see Dwight Clark in the back of the end zone and Joe Montana scrambling to find him.[44] But for a member of the media, it was a shithole. It was cramped, and there was only one elevator. There was also only one bathroom.

At one point, I looked out of our booth down below to the media lunch line and she was there. I leaned in to Aikman and said, "She is down there. I am going to meet her." It's one thing to act like a geeky

---

44. My dad called that play on the radio with Pat Summerall. An autographed picture of Clark making the catch is on a wall of my home office. Take that, San Francisco!

high school kid who has a crush—quite another to do it with Troy Aikman. But there I was.

My plan: Act like I needed coffee. Never mind the Keurig machine in the booth. I hurried to the bathroom and made sure my hair was placed just right. I stood by her and waited for her to turn around as I timed my coffee pour with hers.

I said, "Hi."

She said, "Hi. Talked to Rich Eisen lately?"

I said, "Why? Because I am stalking you through him?"

She laughed and said yes.

I said, "So what's your story?"

This was pretty forward by my standards.

She said, "Well, I live with my boyfriend."

I said, "Well, that's stupid."

That was *really* forward by my standards.

She laughed, and we talked for a minute and that was it. I did the game, then hopped on the cable car that was traveling six miles an hour so FOX could broadcast my trek from one game to the other. That was dumb and insulting to the viewers—acting like they care so much about who is calling the game—but we did it. I walked into AT&T with literally eight minutes to spare—just enough time to open my scorebook, hastily write down the lineups, and get ready to roll.

I think that day would have made my dad proud. He was a workaholic. He never turned down a chance to do a game. I think he would have enjoyed me coming back from my vocal problems to do two games in one day. And he probably would have appreciated that the whole time, all I could think about was a beautiful woman.

———————

Well, I was hooked. My crush from the eye contact had tripled after our brief encounter.

A month later, I was in Green Bay and walked into the auditorium where we held our production meetings with Horn and Pam Oliver, our sideline reporter. The only other person there was Michelle.

I introduced her to Steve by saying, "This is Michelle Beisner, and she stupidly lives with her boyfriend."

She hesitated, and then said, "Well, that may be changing."

Holy wait what hold on now wait huh what?

SO YOU'RE SAYING THERE'S A CHANCE?

Life! Hope! Sunshine! Rainbows! I asked if she wanted to meet for a drink after our respective production dinners. She hesitated and said to call her at the Hilton and leave a message telling her where I would be. This would have been the greatest news of all time, except for one small detail:

She wasn't staying at the Hilton.

She had intentionally told me the wrong hotel so I could not find her, because she was still unsure if her existing relationship was truly ending. It's admirable, when you think about it. It showed her integrity, which I would later learn is as solid as anyone's I know.

Of course, I was not about to sit in my hotel room and admire her integrity. That night at dinner, I kept texting Rich to see if my drink with her was still possible. He was texting her responses to me, and my responses to her, for about fifteen minutes, when he realized he had done enough. He said, "Look, I like you both. You guys work it out."

He gave me her number and gave her mine. That is when the stalking really began.

It started in true twenty-first-century fashion as a texting relationship, a friendship at this point. Nothing crazy. Just fun. I loved her sense of humor. *Beautiful, works in sports, AND funny? What? Tell me she likes porn and I will faint.*

A few weeks later, Michelle was scheduled to work a game in St. Louis. Unfortunately, I was supposed to be back in Green Bay at the same time. Michelle is a foodie. She texted me that she was coming to my city, and did I know any great restaurants that she had to try? I said I did know a few restaurants, but she would only get the names if I got to take her. *Smooth, Joe!*

She agreed . . . as long as she could meet me there.

No, I said. I had to pick her up at her hotel.

She relented, but made it clear it wasn't a date. It was supposed to just be a work dinner, filled with talk about football and the Cover 2 defense. As it turns out, she wanted to meet me at the restaurant so she would have an out. She wanted to be able to leave as soon as the check came, in case I talked too much or smelled of urine.

About seven minutes into our ride to Paul Manno's restaurant, I was already talking way, way too much. I was *unloading*. It was a complete meltdown. I told her everything I ever wanted to tell anyone about my life, and my divorce, and my kids, and my father, and my job. I drove by every house I ever lived in . . . it all came spilling out, fast. I needed a time-out and she needed a snorkel.

But ten minutes into dinner, I knew I had to marry this woman. I cannot explain why. I just knew.

After dinner, we went to the bar at a restaurant called Café Napoli. It was the wrong place. It was packed, and people were coming up to me, and it was awkward. I had my finger in her jean belt loop. She had her hand on my belt. We didn't know each other well at all, but we both knew there was a connection. I couldn't get close enough.

We went to her hotel for another drink. The guy who sings the anthem at St. Louis sporting events was there closing down his spot from his band's night. I introduced Michelle, and then he and I sang "The Star-Spangled Banner" together in the lobby. I had never felt so carefree in my hometown in my life. I didn't care who saw me. I belted it out and made her laugh.

I was all in, immediately.

She was not.

She really was not in a position to start anything with me, and she made that clear, too—frequently. Every reminder was like a slap in the face, but I kept coming back for more. We moved ahead in fits and starts until the Super Bowl in New Orleans. She was there to cover it, and I was there to cover her. Not physically. I was just dying to be near her. Her relationship had officially ended, but now I had to deal with her "mourning" phase.[45]

I didn't consider how our potential relationship would look to the people in our business. I honestly did not care. I was divorced and had been separated for a few years. But she cared. The last time her co-workers saw her in public with a guy, it was someone else. Now she was going to show up at a Super Bowl with an older guy from another network?

---

45. At least, that's what she called it. Dime-store psychology!

Even though we had been aboveboard the whole way, she didn't like how it looked. I understand. It's hard for a woman in this business, and Michelle has fought to establish credibility. She was a Denver Broncos cheerleader from ages twenty to twenty-six, and the cheerleader stereotype follows her wherever she goes. Now she would be dating the guy who calls the Super Bowl at FOX. She did not want to look like a climber.

At event after event that week in New Orleans, everything between us was really difficult. She would go one way and leave me to go another. She was getting looks from some of the people who worked with her. Friends told her that being with me was not good for her career.

That week was one bad night followed by another for me. The highlight, believe it or not, was appearing on Artie Lange's show on DirecTV. They had built him a village for the Super Bowl and I went on and did about forty-five minutes. It is, to this day, one of the two best interviews anyone has ever done with me. (The other was *Center-Stage* with Michael Kay for the YES Network.)

I left New Orleans a beaten man. I felt lost. We had had moments where we were so close and shared some things that were really deep, but the public side of it was too much for her. I went home before the game to a Super Bowl party at my house that my sister organized. It was not a big party, but it was more than I could handle. I just wanted to go to bed. I was not a good host.

Michelle and I agreed that we would take a time-out. We would stop the daily texts and phone calls that had meant so much to me. We broke up before we ever really started dating.

But then . . . then: She called me the next day and said, "I can't *not* talk to you." I felt the same way.

A couple of weeks later, I flew to Los Angeles to pick her up and take her to Laguna Niguel. On the flight, I had an epiphany:

I'm a chump.

I was doing all the chasing. You can't build a relationship that way. When I landed in LA, I called my mom first and the airline second. I told my mom this didn't feel right. The courtship was too one-sided, and I was going home. I called Kate Hudson to talk about it, and stopped by Jason Patric's house, which was near Michelle's apartment. Both of them agreed this wasn't a good way to start a relationship.

I went to Michelle's. She opened the door and gave me a big hug.

I said, "It's good to see you. I'm leaving."

She thought I was joking. I wasn't. She asked me to stay, but I wouldn't. It felt good to say no. Not as desperate. Smarter.

I had a few hours to kill before my flight home. I went straight to a bar called O'Brien's in Santa Monica, just blocks from where she lived. She was texting and calling me, begging me to stay. I ignored her for the first time since I met her. I talked instead to this guy from Mississippi about college football at the bar, for what felt like two hours over beers. It was probably closer to forty-five minutes.

I finally texted her back. I told her I was at O'Brien's and about to leave. Within minutes, she was there. She ran into my arms.

After all those months, she had chased me.

We stayed there in Santa Monica and went on our first real "date." We played pool. We had dinner. We laughed next to a Dumpster in a parking lot behind the restaurant on a perfect night. It didn't matter where we were. We were together in every sense.

Chapter 18

The Mountaintop

During the 2012 football season, I got an e-mail singing the praises of an organization called WorldServe International, which provides clean water to people in Africa. The effort was spearheaded by a guy named Doug Pitt. You may have heard of Doug's brother, Brad.[46]

Doug and I met in Clayton, a suburb of St. Louis, and talked for about an hour. He and some NFL players were climbing Mount Kilimanjaro to raise awareness and money for clean water wells in Masai villages in Tanzania, and he wanted me to document it.

I was interested in helping. I had no interest in climbing. I am not

---

46. This is true. Doug actually is Brad Pitt's brother. This has absolutely nothing to do with the story, and I have never met Brad Pitt, but I just went and dropped his name anyway. I am unstoppable!

an outdoorsman—if you see me going for a hike, I am probably look-ing for my golf ball. But at the very end of our conversation, after we had talked about our children, Doug said, "Hey, why don't you climb it with your sixteen-year-old? We have room and I am sure she would enjoy being a part of this experience."

That changed my view. Natalie was a junior in high school. Time was already slipping away. When would I get the chance to spend two weeks in Africa with her, trying to climb one of the world's tallest summits?

I told Doug we would do it. The girls and I had been through so much. They always knew they came first for me. From those early days of reading Toot and Puddle books to them in bed, or lying on the floor, making dumb Ken and Barbie voices while we played, I have been theirs. I knew I was on solid ground with them even in the dark-est days of my divorce.

I just wanted to go far away with Natalie, with no distractions. (I would have loved to have taken Trudy, too, but she was too young.) It was one of the best decisions I have ever made. From our training to the conversation and anticipation, Natalie and I had a blast.

Truthfully, even after I said yes, I did not think I could do it. I see people running marathons and marvel at someone's ability to run twenty-six-plus miles on pavement up- and downhill. I have a better chance of sprouting wings and flying than ever doing one of those. Endurance is not my thing. But this was different. I wanted to prove to myself that I could do it, and I wanted to do it with Natalie.

The only problem was that, between committing to the climb and the climb itself, I had met Michelle. Now I was leaving the country for two weeks as our romance was beginning.

A two-week trip does not sound long. I think we've had commercial breaks during the Super Bowl that lasted that long. But when you go all the way to Africa, and you leave behind a burgeoning relationship, two weeks feels like an eternity. I was already worried about the distance from Los Angeles to St. Louis. Now I was on the other side of the world, in a country where cell phone towers aren't exactly dotting the landscape.

When Natalie and I arrived at our hotel in Tanzania, we went to the lobby bar. I wanted a beer, and Natalie was probably hoping for chicken fingers and a Coke. In a small-world moment, we happened to run into Chris Long at the bar. Chris is a defensive end for the St. Louis Rams and the son of my FOX colleague, Howie. I have known Chris since before he played in the NFL. He was sitting with another Ram, James Hall.

Chris and James had just finished climbing Kilimanjaro.

He said, "Bro, that was the hardest thing I have ever done in my life."

I'm sorry . . . *what?!?!?* You're Chris Long! You play in the NFL! You have muscles in your earlobes! Did you really just call what I am about to do with my sixteen-year-old daughter the *hardest thing you have ever done in your life?*

Natalie and I looked at each other and said, "We have NO CHANCE." We almost headed to the airport.

But we stayed. We had a couple of nights in the hotel before our safari and climb. The hotel had Wi-Fi, which meant I could use my iPad to chat with Michelle. I would make sure Natalie was set in bed, then head to the lobby to try and corral this woman I clearly adored while she straddled the fence thousands of miles away.

Natalie and I left to help deliver a water well to a Masai village. Then we did our safari in the Ngorongoro Crater. Then it was time for our climb.

If you ever climb Kilimanjaro, a little advice:

1. Do not ask Chris Long if it's hard.
2. Get malaria shots before you fly to Africa.
3. Pick up a prescription for a drug called Diamox.

Diamox is a necessity, especially for first-time climbers. This drug oxygenates your blood while the air gets thinner up the mountain. Natalie had a bad reaction to the amount of Diamox she was taking. It knocked her out before we even started. She can be a little dramatic sometimes, so I told her to suck it up and stop complaining. But she was really sick. Let me take this opportunity to say here, in my book: I'm sorry, Natalie.

I was also told that I should carry Cialis with me in my pack in case my blood oxygen got low. So I bought some Cialis, too. I have never bought that before or since—even though I have been taking Propecia since the day it came on the market, I don't have any of the sexual side effects that I have read about online. I didn't want to actually take the Cialis. Nobody wants to climb a mountain hunched over, and it would be awkward to call my doctor and tell him I was on top of Mount Kilimanjaro and I had an erection lasting more than four hours, and anyway the call probably would not have gone through because the farther we got from civilization, the less my phone worked.

I was on Verizon, and their coverage at that time on Kilimanjaro was not great. Chris Danforth, a fellow climber, had AT&T. When I called Michelle from his phone, it sounded like I was calling from New Jersey. I begged Chris to use his phone when our climb shut down each day. He let me, and while I was climbing this huge rock, I felt I was also making progress with Michelle. After our third full day of climbing, I was wandering around camp, looking into Kenya, when Michelle told me she had been at a friend's wedding in Los Angeles and wished I had been there as her date. For the first time, she sounded wistful while we chatted, and I marked that moment in time. Things were turning.

Here I was, climbing a mountain at the age of forty-three, something I never thought in my wildest dreams I would even attempt, with my daughter. Meanwhile, I was still chasing down this woman who had given me hope.

I made it to the top. Unfortunately, Natalie did not. That overprescription sunk her. But I am more proud of her than I am of myself, for two reasons.

First: She really tried. She got to about 16,000 feet before our guide thought it was a health risk for her to continue. She fought, and she had to be told to stop. I think what she accomplished was a lot more impressive than climbing the whole 19,000 feet while healthy.

Second: When our guide told her to stop climbing, I said, "Nat, we did our best. Let's get you down safely." I will never forget her response. "Dad, the only way this is going to be bad is if *you* don't make it to the top. Go! I'll be fine."

And I did. I went on. I saw the sunrise from the top of the mountain. You don't spend a lot of time at the top. It's like Clark Griswold and the Grand Canyon. You look, you nod, you snap some pictures, and you head back down with a raging headache. However, for that one brief moment, looking down at the clouds and a glacier is breathtaking. It is easily the prettiest sight I have ever seen . . . except one. That came when I got back to our base camp and saw Natalie. She popped up off the cot she was sleeping on, with tears in her eyes, proud of what her father had done.

That hit me. After all those years of trying to make everybody else happy, especially my girls, I realized how much they want *me* to be happy. And when you realize that, you realize that it's OK to try to make yourself happy. It isn't selfish.

That week on that mountain reminded me of how small I really am. Life goes on. I can't protect my girls from every hardship that comes their way. But I can show them how to plow through whatever comes their way. That's how they've been raised. Staying in an unhappy marriage would have been easy. Giving up on Michelle would have been easy. Saying no to Doug Pitt would have been easy. Turning away after we talked to Chris Long would have been easy. Making it to the summit and taking in the view at 19,000 feet gave me great satisfaction. I was truly happy. I had not felt that way in a long time.

Chapter 19

So What!

I've become more content with who I am since I met Michelle. I feel supported by her and by Natalie and Trudy. I can do my job the way I think it should be done, and not worry about anything else.

I keep finding new challenges professionally. Sometimes, the challenges find me. FOX has a golf package now, which is completely new to all of us. Golf is a very different animal from football or baseball. It's really like broadcasting dozens of sporting events at the same time—I sit in the same tower, and we go from one golfer to another, and I'm supposed to know what everybody is doing.[47]

---

47. The day that FOX bought a golf package, before I even knew I would be involved, ESPN's Mike Tirico texted me and offered to help in any way. The week before FOX's first US Open, Tirico sent me all his notes from the previous year's Open. That's an exceptionally nice thing to do.

For the 2015 US Open at Chambers Bay, I didn't see one shot live. We were too far away, and my back was facing the course. I just looked at one screen after another, listened to what I was told in my earpiece, and managed the broadcast. It's good training for being an air-traffic controller.

I also have a new show for DirecTV called *Undeniable.* I interview famous athletes, and we talk about their life journeys, successes, failures, and regrets. It's been a joy, and it might be the best-received work of my career. Derek Jeter felt so comfortable during my interview, he brought up the report that he gave gift baskets to women who slept with him. I had great interviews with Troy, Abby Wambach, and Michael Phelps.

Undeniable lets me show my personality while getting to crack the outer shell of some of our era's greatest athletes before a studio audience of around two hundred people. Seeing Troy Aikman emote on that stage felt like an accomplishment. He wanted to have something like that recorded for his daughters, and this was his spot to lay it all out there. Troy is one of my best friends now, and doing that show with him was a highlight for me.

I took the lessons from *Joe Buck Live* and applied them to *Undeniable.* It's not live, so we can edit it down, the way many talk shows are edited. We have a clear vision. It's been extremely satisfying. Viewers have been more positive about *Undeniable* than any work I have done in a long time, but here is the great thing: I don't obsess over that anymore.

I know I can't change everybody's minds, and it's futile to try. Viewers still give me a hard time about Randy Moss, as though we have some deep personal hatred for each other. In reality, I made one comment on the air eleven years ago.

Besides, Moss and I were coworkers for a while. He did analysis for FOX before leaving for ESPN. When we hired him, I introduced him on the air and said, "We good?"

He said, "I played the game, you analyzed it. You said what you said, I did what I did, and we moved on."

That was it. I've been on Artie Lange's radio show and wrote the foreword to one of his books, but people still yell his name at me sometimes, like I'm going to cry or something.

I've learned to put all that aside and appreciate the cool moments we experience in this business. Even though I'm not a fan of any team, it's fun to be on the inside of the sports world and see what really happens.[48]

Sometimes I get a feel for how a game will go before it starts. Before the Super Bowl in 2011, I watched the Packers and Steelers practice and became convinced that the Packers would win. They were just in a better frame of mind. Their practices were crisper.

And I really think I knew who was going to win Super Bowl XLVIII in New Jersey in 2014 before the coin was flipped. The Broncos were playing the Seahawks, and a lot of people figured Peyton Manning and Denver would win.

The Broncos' practice was fine, and Peyton was great with us in our production meeting, as he always is. He is smart, he is so polished, and he knows how to answer questions.

---

48. I am an unabashed fan of the St. Louis Blues. I own season tickets. But I don't do hockey games on the air. I'm not smart enough—the game is too fast, and the names are too long.

But then we had our production meeting with the Seahawks. We sat in the room with the Legion of Boom, their defensive backs: Kam Chancellor, Earl Thomas, Richard Sherman, Byron Maxwell, and Walter Thurmond. And every question we asked, they answered with this ridiculously high level of confidence.

Sherman was known as the big talker, and Thomas is a big talker, too, but they all deferred to Chancellor. He'd say: "Anybody comes over the middle, I'm going to take their fucking head off." The other guys said: "Kam's the intimidator, not them. If they come over the middle, Kam will take care of it."

Sherman said Denver's receivers didn't scare him. Now, part of that is an act. I understand. But it wasn't *all* an act. Earl Thomas was hyperactive, ready to jump out of the room. I didn't want to look at Chancellor wrong because I felt like he might step up and punch me. And Sherman is so smart, and he is fearless. They were saying, "We don't care what Peyton Manning does at the line of scrimmage. He can say 'Omaha!' five hundred times. He can move guys around. We're not moving." That's how they played their defense all year. They stayed in their base defense and shut you down.

I went back to Manhattan and saw Michelle in the hotel room. She grew up in Denver. I said, "I'm telling you right now, your Broncos have no chance in that game." The Seahawks beat the Broncos 43–8, and I wasn't surprised. I had never felt so sure about any game I had ever done.

Before Game 7 of the 2014 World Series, we were talking with Giants manager Bruce Bochy. Bruce is a great guy. I won't say he likes me better than he liked my dad, but I think he appreciates that, unlike my dad, I never punted a football into his nuts.

Bochy has always been so honest with us. He knows we know what we can say on the air that day and what we can't.

The question going into this game would be Giants ace Madison Bumgarner. He was available to come out of the bullpen on two days' rest, but nobody knew how long he could go. So we asked Bochy, "What's the most you could get out of him?"

Bochy said, "I can't see us getting more than two innings out of him. Maybe three innings at the most."

Bumgarner pitched five innings that night and finished the game. It was one of the greatest performances I have ever seen in any sport. And I think our broadcast was better because we could confidently tell viewers, "This is way more than Bruce Bochy expected." We knew from our history with him that he wasn't playing a game with us. He expected two, maybe three innings. And here was Bumgarner in his fifth inning on the mound, in the ninth inning of a 2–1 Game 7 of the World Series. He was that good.

When McCarver was in his last year with FOX, in 2013, we did some interviews together. We always enjoyed doing them together because he would answer a question, and then I would make fun of whatever he said, and we would both laugh. After one interview, Tim and I reflected a little bit, which is not something guys normally do in a broadcast booth.

In the eighteen years we had worked together, we had never really talked about Tim working with my dad, other than that first brief conversation in a bar when we were paired up. But as we talked, Tim turned to me and said:

"You know, I never told you something after all these years. I remember a time when you came to visit us in the booth. Your dad said, 'Hey, say hi to Tim.' And you looked at me like you wanted to kill me."

I knew *exactly* what he was talking about. I remember the moment. I remember being in that booth. And Tim was right: I wanted to punch him in the face. I wanted to say, "Hey, my dad is working his ass off and trying to make this work, and he is sixty-five years old! Can't you work with him? It could be good! Can't you engage?" I just kind of glared at him and moved on.

But when Tim brought it up, I had no interest in revisiting it. I said, "I don't know why I would have done that or looked that way." I wasn't going to get into all the old slights: *Back then you said you can't see the wind, you can see the effect of the wind* . . . I just let it go. By this point, I was proud to say Tim was my friend. The scars had disappeared. The end of our last broadcast, after Game 6 of the 2013 World Series, was one of the most emotional moments of my career. I got to say good-bye to a broadcasting legend, and a man who had become a dear friend.

My father has been gone for fourteen years, but if you've lost a beloved parent, you understand: He is with me every day. And even in death, he is an outsize personality in St. Louis. Strangers still tell me stories about him. He has a star on the St. Louis Walk of Fame, in the loop area on Delmar in St. Louis. It's in front of this restaurant where I often take my girls: Snarf's. We always walk by and give a little look.

I've carried on a lot of his traditions just because I feel it's my duty.

He hosted a police prayer breakfast every year, so I host a police prayer breakfast every year. He helped this charity and that charity, so I will help this charity and that charity. I keep doing what he would expect me to do.

Sometimes, I still feel like the fat kid who can't fit into a batboy's uniform. But I'm proud that I've taken care of myself. I obsess about it. I do some weird stuff to keep myself in shape. Every morning I put grass-fed pure butter in my coffee. It's evidently a good fat that you need in the morning to kind of get yourself going. You laugh. You might want to throw up. But that's my breakfast. It keeps me full until noon every day.

I knew when Michelle and I got married that people would draw the wrong conclusions about us. They would say I left my wife for Michelle, or that I found a much younger woman, or that she married me to help her career, which would be insane. Michelle is seven years younger than I am, which really isn't that much. My parents were fourteen years apart, so my dad was twice the cradle robber I am.

The truth is that we are best friends. I'm just so lucky that she came into my life when I felt broken and rudderless.

Michelle works now at ESPN as a feature reporter and host. I could not be more proud of her. She is a hard worker who proves her integrity with every assignment. And like with my father, I never have to worry when someone tells me that they have worked with my wife. People love working with her.

It must be hard to see your dad fall in love with a woman who is not your mom. But Natalie and Trudy have always known that I put them first, and they see how happy I am. I rarely lose my temper, and if I do, they just laugh at me. They know it will pass. And Michelle is a great role model for them. They are old enough that she can just be their friend. They already have a mother. They don't need another one.

In the spring of 2013, I drove forty-five minutes to Troy, Missouri, to get my first tattoos. I didn't want them to be prominent. I think I would look pretty dumb with sleeves of tattoos, and I don't think FOX executives would have been happy if I got that Mike Tyson thing on my face. But I got two tattoos I really wanted.

The tattoo artist said, "This is going to hurt a little bit." So I braced for pain. And when needle hit skin, I thought: "This is NOTHING." If you want to feel pain, have somebody put needles into your head, and have them scalp you and take a strip of hair out of the back of your head and start planting it in the front of your head. THAT hurts. This little thing that I felt on my arm was a minor nuisance.

After all these hair-replacement surgeries, I'm hardened. I think I'd be a good prison guard.

On my right arm, I got the word *Bastante*, which is Spanish for *enough*. I wanted to remind myself: Enough worrying about your divorce. Enough worrying about nameless, faceless people who rip you. I have come to see that everyone in my position gets ripped—it's not just me. Michelle always tells me, "Quiet your mind." I look at that *Bastante* tattoo in the morning and remember to quiet my mind.

The other meaning of *Bastante* is: I can't love my kids enough. I can't enjoy my job enough. I can find infinite joy in these things.

On my left arm, I got two words. They are the same two words on the bracelet that my dad gave my mom when I was little:

So what!

My mom gave her *So what!* bracelet to my daughter Natalie, who has a tendency to worry. Natalie wears it all the time. Now I have a tattoo that says the same thing. I guess it's become a bit of a family motto.

I didn't tell anybody I was getting tattoos. Nobody would have believed me anyway. I was embarrassed to show my kids. Natalie was in high school, and she said, "What the hell? What are you doing? Are you, like, having a breakdown? A midlife crisis?" She was looking at Michelle, who has two tattoos, and Michelle said, "I had nothing to do with this. I'm just learning about this today, when you are." My mom was stunned, too.

And you know what? That's one of the reasons I got them: I'm in my forties, and I don't need anybody's approval. If they think I'm being foolish, so what? They will get over it.

I'm in a good place. I'm comfortable with myself, my career, and my life. I don't care if you think I'm a spoiled kid who is only employed because of my dad, or if you think I hate your team. I do the best I can.

And I don't care if the only story you remember from this whole book is about my hair.

By the way: I color it, too.